Praise for
Living Well, Spending Less

Living Well, Spending Less is an inspiring book full of step-by-step instructions and spiritual wisdom. I love how Ruth is transparent about her mistakes as she leads us to reevaluate our priorities. This book is a great biblical guide to living well and finding joy!

> COURTNEY JOSEPH, author of *Women Living Well* (the book) and *WomenLivingWell.org* (the blog)

In this book, you will be inspired by Ruth's authenticity and honesty as she shares her own journey from constantly spending time and money chasing after more to discovering she already has all the makings of a rich and full life right where she's at. If you struggle to simplify your life and wish you could savor the here and now, this book is a must-read.

> CRYSTAL PAINE, founder of MoneySavingMom.com and *New York Times* bestselling author of *Say Goodbye to Survival Mode*

Ruth's book inspires, motivates, and comforts at the same time. Her book is about far more than saving money; it's about learning how to be content and satisfied, regardless of your financial situation. It made me wish Ruth lived down the street so I could meet her for coffee and a chat.

> STEPHANIE NELSON, founder of CouponMom.com

Ruth Soukup knows firsthand how mamas like us live crazy busy lives, and she steps in as a friend to help us manage and love every minute of it. In *Living Well, Spending Less*, Ruth offers her best tips for gaining control over the chaos with wisdom-based insights on all things thrifty and family. I'll be reading it again and again and recommending it to friends who long to live and love the good life that God has for them!

> RENEE SWOPE, bestselling author of *A Confident Heart* (book and devotional) and Proverbs 31 Ministries' radio cohost of *"Everyday Life" with Lysa & Renee*

It doesn't take more than a trip to Target or a glance at *People* magazine for me to come face-to-face with my own insatiable desire for *more*. More beauty. More designer clothes. More gadgets. *More happy*. But, as Ruth Soukup discloses through her signature honest and down-to-earth style, "more" will never make you and me "full." But here's the good news: The life you crave is far closer than you can imagine. Ruth will show you how to get there.

> MICHELE CUSHATT, speaker and author of *Undone*

Living Well, Spending Less is relatable and helpful without being condemning. Ruth takes a complicated, emotionally laden issue like spending and makes it seem possible to come to terms with what's keeping us stuck both in our finances and in our lives.

> EDIE WADSWORTH, author of *Coming Home* and blogger at Lifeingrace

Ruth Soukup has learned contentment does not come with a Pottery Barn label. Every woman who struggles with wanting more should read this book before she discovers a stack of receipts and a trail of regrets. It's never too late, as Ruth so engagingly and shares, to discover that the Good Life— God's best—is free.

GLYNNIS WHITWER, author and executive director of communications at Proverbs 31 Ministries

I couldn't stop reading *Living Well, Spending Less*. I tried to —only because I had other things I needed to do—but I couldn't. Rarely is there a book so adept at weaving personal story with practical tips. I found myself craving this good life that Ruth writes of—a life that is possible for anyone who reads this book.

EMILY T. WIERENGA (WWW.EMILYWIERENGA), author of the bestselling memoir *Atlas Girl*

Living Well, Spending Less is about more than planning a better budget or maintaining an organized home; it offers tips for easing stress and improving time management. Here, Ruth gifts us with a simple yet powerful blueprint for realizing true, deep contentment with all of the good things that this life has to offer.

KASEY KNIGHT TRENUM, blogger at time2saveworkshops.com

Living Well, Spending Less is an incredible book that will teach you how to spend smart without compromising a great life. Ruth's stories and practical advice will make you want to be a better mother, wife, sister, and friend. Trust me, you'll be happy you read this book.

RACHEL CRUZE, coauthor with Dave Ramsey of *Smart Money Smart Kids*

LIVING WELL
Spending Less

LIVING WELL

Spending Less

12 SECRETS of the *Good Life*

RUTH SOUKUP

ZONDERVAN

Living Well, Spending Less
Copyright © 2014 by Ruth Soukup

This title is also available as a Zondervan ebook.
Visit www.zondervan.com/ebooks.

Requests for information should be addressed to:
Zondervan, 3900 *Sparks Dr. SE, Grand Rapids, Michigan 49546*

Library of Congress Cataloging-in-Publication Data

Soukup, Ruth, 1978 –
    Living well, spending less : 12 secrets of the good life / Ruth Soukup.
        pages cm
      ISBN 978-0-310-33767-6 (paperback)
        1. Finance, Personal. 2. Budgets, Personal. 3. Saving and investment.
    I. Title.
    IIG179.S55255   2014
    650.1 – dc23   2014011390

Published in association with The Fedd Agency, P.O. Box 341973, Austin, TX
78734.

Cover design: Dual Identity
Interior design: Beth Shagene

First Printing November 2014 / Printed in the United States of America

To Chuck, Maggie, and Annie—
thank you for always reminding me
what the Good Life is really about

Contents

PART TWO: SPENDING LESS

Introduction

Once every couple of weeks, I interrupt my normally predictable morning routine and drive thirty minutes south to the city of Fort Myers to do a live three-minute segment on the local CBS affiliate. Sometimes I'll share my best tips for saving on groceries; other times it will be advice on how to get your budget back on track or suggestions for some great handmade gift ideas. And every time I go on the air, it never ceases to make me pause when I hear myself being introduced as the WINK News money-saving expert.

A money-saving expert.

Oh, the irony.

It doesn't stop there. Over the past few years I have been awarded with other similar titles: *Coupon Girl*, *Super Saver*, *Deal Pro*, and *Savings Star*. Never in a million years would I have chosen one of those words to describe myself. The reality is that I am less a money-*saving* expert than a money-*spending* expert. I excel in the fine art of shopping when I shouldn't, and buying just for the thrill of it. This particular expertise has gotten me in a lot of trouble over the years, so it is no accident that this book—and my blog of the same name — is titled Living Well *Spending Less* and not Living Well *Saving More*.

Until I started my blog, *LivingWellSpendingLess.com*, the word *frugality* didn't really exist in my vocabulary. I grew up in a family where money was never an issue. From the outside, it probably looked as though we had everything. But privilege comes with a price, and the reality was far from perfect. During my senior year of college, my carefully crafted world came crashing down, and for the next two years I lived in a world of darkness and depression.

I very nearly died, and my survival was nothing short of a miracle; I was just too blind to see it right away. Over the next ten years I attended (then dropped out of) law school, got married, moved cross-country three times, and had two children. During these ten years of nearly constant change, pretty much the only thing that stayed consistent in my life was the mall. And Amazon.com. And Target. Pottery Barn. Williams-Sonoma. Gymboree. I filled our life with stuff, but it never filled the void.

But God had a plan for even a broken shopaholic like me.

Sometimes grace is shaped like a coupon.

These days, I'm passionate about saving money not because I think I've got this personal finance thing all figured out; on the contrary — as I sit here drinking an overpriced cup of designer coffee — I still make financial mistakes every single day. I'm months behind on my filing system. I struggle to stay within my budget. I neglect balancing my checkbook. I spend money on things I shouldn't. And every single month I procrastinate paying my bills.

I am far from perfect.

Thankfully, God hasn't called me to be perfect.

Through this journey toward financial peace, I have found that the state of my finances usually mirrors the state of the rest of my life. If I am a mess with my money, then I am generally a mess everywhere else. Thus, I am passionate about saving money, not because I have all the answers, but because I have learned that money—whether too much of it or too little—permeates every area, every single facet, of our lives. It is directly connected to our spiritual, emotional, and even physical well-being. Ultimately, how we spend our money is a direct reflection of what is in our hearts.

In the end, this book is far more than just a money-saving guide or a simple collection of financial dos and don'ts. This book is about *living well* and spending less. It is based on the hard-fought lessons learned through both my own mistakes and my own successes. Because I'm a Christian, it is also based on what the Bible has taught me about the Good Life, and as such, it includes some Bible verses.

My hope and prayer is that you will be challenged as you read this book—challenged to reevaluate your priorities and make the necessary changes that will result not only in a bigger bank account but in a better life, one filled with contentment and meaning and joy. It won't be easy—lasting change is hard work—but please trust me when I tell you the rewards are worth the effort.

The Good Life is waiting for you. Are you ready to find it?

PART ONE

Living Well

The Good Life Is Not What We Think It Is

Not life, but good life, is to be chiefly valued.

Socrates, quoted by Plato in *Crito*

"Do not store up for yourselves treasures on earth, where moths and vermin destroy, and where thieves break in and steal. But store up for yourselves treasure in heaven … For where your treasure is, there your heart will be also."

Matthew 6:19 – 21

To laugh often and much; to win the respect of intelligent people and the affection of children; to earn the appreciation of honest critics and endure the betrayal of false friends; to appreciate beauty; to find the best in others; to leave the world a bit better, whether by a healthy child, a garden patch, or a redeemed social condition; to know even one life has breathed easier because you have lived. This is to have succeeded.

Ralph Waldo Emerson

There I sat, a little girl tucked away in my secret hiding place — a hidden crawl space nestled behind the closet of one of the many but rarely used guest rooms in our sprawling 1930s colonial. No one bothered me there, and in that hideaway I spent countless hours in my own world of make-believe, losing myself in the elaborate game I'd made up of creating my dream house.

It was a meticulous, time-consuming process. I'd start by picking out the biggest, most ostentatious mansion for sale in the real estate section of my father's latest copy of *Architectural Digest* — the one with the formal English garden in front and the cliff overlooking the ocean in back, available for the bargain price of only $17 million. I'd then take a sheet of graph paper snatched from my dad's desk drawer and carefully sketch out my dream version of what I thought the floor plan should look like.

I was always careful to include such "basic" necessities as an indoor pool, a basketball court, and a game room. My perfect house always included at least ten bedrooms, with a fireplace, sitting room, and cavernous spa-like bathroom in each. There were at least two gourmet kitchens (you never know when you might need an extra), a dining room that seated forty, a university-sized library filled with books from floor to ceiling, and every other far-fetched amenity my eleven-year-old imagination — inspired mostly by the Barbie Dreamhouse and too much time spent watching *Life-styles of the Rich and Famous*—could conjure up.

When the floor plan was finally complete—and it always took *hours* to get the blueprint just right—I'd decorate. I'd pull out the thick stack of department store catalogs I had pilfered from the recycle pile and spend countless *more* hours methodically picking out furniture, linens, and accessories for every single room, right down to the china dishes in the cabinets, the fluffy towels in the bathroom, and the classy shoes in the closet.

As I'd shop the catalogs, I'd picture my adorable, well-dressed children and my kind, handsome, and wildly successful husband. I'd envision our enchanted, problem-free existence, the happy times we'd spend enjoying our luxurious home.

However, when I had finally exhausted every catalog and filled every imaginary room with as much expensive "stuff" as I could possibly find, I was never left with a feeling of accomplishment, despite all the time and effort I had exerted. On the contrary, the letdown was intense. I filled and filled and filled, but it always left me empty. And so I would start over with a new house and a new floor plan, ensuring countless more hours of wanting and dreaming and filling, knowing that this time—*finally*—I would get it right.

In my dream house, life was perfect. In my dream house, I was happy.

Or so I thought.

What I didn't know then was that even at that tender age I was developing a dangerous habit. I had already begun equating possessions with happiness. I had already started believing that a Good Life was dependent on what I had. At eleven years old I was convinced that if I could just get the right *stuff*, my life would be complete. Full. Happy. Satisfied.

This destructive pattern would set the tone for much of my adult life and nearly destroy my marriage. Of course, I didn't learn just how destructive that way of thinking truly was until much, much later.

The Grown-Up Dream House

After so many years of merely dreaming about it, I was more than ready for the chance to be all grown-up, and to remodel and decorate my *real* dream house, albeit on a *slightly* smaller scale.

Finally the day came, though admittedly not under the happiest of circumstances. In 2004, our home was severely damaged by Hurricane Charley. Afterward, my husband, Chuck, and I decided to make some major renovations beyond just the necessary repairs from the hurricane damage. Chuck—the financial rock of our family—insisted on paying cash. After using insurance money to fix the broken roof and windows, we began saving to remodel the inside.

While I (not so) patiently waited, I collected ideas. Once again, I'd spend hours drooling over magazines and catalogs, tearing out pictures of all the things I liked, all the things I knew I wouldn't be able to live without, all the things I knew would make me happy.

Just like I planned as a little girl, in my grown-up dream house life would be perfect.

After what seemed like forever, the big moment finally arrived, and our much-anticipated remodeling project began. There were fresh coats of paint and new walls, a library of my very own, custom cabinetry with pullout shelves, granite countertops, new hardwood and real stone floors, gorgeous new curtains and rugs and furniture and accessories. But then, before we knew it, the projects were done and the money we had set aside was completely gone.

Except I couldn't stop.

Just like in my childhood game, the letdown was almost more than I could bear. We had spent all this time and money and energy creating the perfect house that I'd always dreamed of, and yet still my life was far from perfect. I still felt unfulfilled. Unsatisfied. Discontent. I still craved more.

And so? I kept shopping. Bored and restless, I'd head to Target or Pottery Barn or Williams-Sonoma searching for something else to fill the void. Over and over I'd fall in love with one trinket or another: the perfect bright-colored throw pillow, shiny picture frame, or earthy coffee mug, or yet another time-saving, semi-automatic floor mop.

The truth is that I had *always* shopped a bit too much, but this was different. My heart would begin to pound and I'd feel a rush of adrenaline as I placed it in my cart, knowing — just knowing — that this was it! *This* was the item that would change my life, make me ecstatic and bring bliss, perfection, and contentment. *This* would finally leave me satisfied.

The rush was replaced with dread and regret as I'd walk through the front door, arms once again filled with shopping bags, and see the look — a mixture of anger, disappointment, and even a little fear — on Chuck's face. "Just stop!" he would scream. "It's enough! We don't need it. You can't do this anymore!"

I couldn't bring myself to admit he might be right, even though deep down I knew I had a problem. I couldn't find a way to make him understand that what I wanted more than anything was to be *full*. So instead I crammed our house full of things. Not surprisingly, the battles got uglier and angrier, until one day we both finally decided we'd had enough. Something had to give.

More Is Never Enough

This idea that more *stuff* will make us happy was not unique to my situation. On the contrary, this message is constantly reinforced at every turn in our consumer-driven society. There is an underlying whisper in every television commercial, every billboard, every magazine spread that taunts us, tempts us, and sucks us in:

If your house looks like this, you'll be satisfied.
If you drive this car, you'll be successful.
If you use this makeup, you'll be beautiful.
If you wear these clothes, you'll be enviable.
If you use this tablet, you'll be organized.
If you eat this food, you'll be skinny.
If your child has this toy, he'll be content.
This will be the thing that changes your life.
This will be the thing that fills you up.

We see the ads, read the magazines and blogs, and even spend hours poring over stunningly perfect images on Pinterest. We see the glamorous, extravagant lives of celebrities and reality stars glorified and immortalized in weekly magazines and on television.

We listen to the whispers as we watch everyone around us filling their lives with more things, prettier things, better things than what we currently have. We want bigger houses, better cars, newer phones, more accessories and clothing and shoes and toys and gadgets and whatever else we decide will usher in the Good Life.

But it never ever does. The whispers are a lie. Lean in, friends, because I have something to tell you: The Good Life is not what we think it is.

You see, stuff in and of itself is not evil. We all need a place to live, clothes to wear, and food to eat. I think it is okay—even natural—to want our home and clothing to look nice, reflecting our personalities and sense of style. Money and possessions on their own are not necessarily harmful or destructive. However, the pursuit of them can be.

Over and over, the Bible warns against this phenomenon:

"Watch out! Be on your guard against all kinds of greed; life does not consist in an abundance of possessions."

LUKE 12:15

Keep your lives free from the love of money and be content with what you have, because God has said, "Never will I leave you; never will I forsake you."

HEBREWS 13:5

"No one can serve two masters. Either you will hate the one and love the other, or you will be devoted to the one and despise the other. You cannot serve both God and money."

LUKE 16:13

I used to think these verses applied only to those who were *actually* wealthy. In my mind, I was off the hook. *Too bad for those rich people*, I thought to myself. *They are out of luck.* It didn't occur to me that the Bible wasn't warning *them*; it was warning *me*. Because while I may not have been rich, I wanted to live like I was. I wanted the best of everything, and even if I couldn't afford the best of everything, I certainly *wished* I could.

In 1 Timothy 6:9–10 (ESV), Paul writes, "Those who *desire* to get rich fall into temptation, into a snare, into many senseless and harmful desires that plunge people into ruin and destruction. For the love of money is a root of all kinds of evils. It is through this *craving* that some have wandered away from the faith and pierced themselves with many pangs" (emphasis mine).

It is not the wealth—or the stuff—that kills us; it is the wanting, the longing, the absolutely insatiable desire for wealth, possessions, power, and status that eventually take over our hearts and minds, leaving room for little else. Whether or not we can afford it is totally irrelevant. What matters is the desire of our heart. Regardless of the never-quite-enough message society wants to give us, a life consumed by always wanting more is *not* the Good Life.

In Search of the Good Life

Desperate times call for desperate measures. After our remodel, as my spending spiraled totally out of control, my husband and I were literally on the brink of divorce. Exhausted by all the fighting and truly willing to do *any-*

thing to save my marriage, I agreed to try something new. We established separate bank accounts and a strict budget, and I agreed to what was essentially an allowance from my husband. I would get a set amount of money each month to be used for groceries, clothing, and household items, and when it was gone, it was gone. I had no choice but to stop spending.

That is, I had no choice but to stop spending *as much*.

Panicked by the thought of giving up what had become an unstoppable need to buy things, I quickly realized I could make my budget stretch much further by saving on food. I learned how to use coupons and was able to cut my monthly grocery bill from $1,000 a month to about $200, leaving me an extra $800 to spend each month on all the *stuff*, on all the pretty things I still thought I needed.

I then began looking for ways to stretch my budget dollars even further, combing the clearance racks for killer deals and taking advantage of Amazon lightning deals several times a day.

I channeled my newfound passion for using coupons, saving money, and finding great deals into a blog I called *Living Well Spending Less*. My original tagline for the blog was "The adventure of finding style and luxury on a budget," and the first line of my introduction read, "I like nice things. My husband hates the price tag."

My goal was simply to stretch my budget so I could buy all the things I wanted. There was no higher noble purpose. On the contrary, to me it was just simple math: the less I spent on food, the more I could spend on shoes (and on everything else). There was still so *much* I wanted, so many pretty things out there *just waiting* for me to take them home. I began shopping for more bargains and became an expert at finding incredible deals on groceries, clothing, and other household goods, but I was still shopping, still buying, still trying to fill that void.

From a financial standpoint, being forced to stick to a strict allowance made a huge difference for our family budget. At the very least, I was no longer sinking us with my spending. But I was still drowning us in things we didn't need.

Eventually, though, as I continued to write about saving money and sought to be a better homemaker, all this stuff I was bringing in started to feel oppressive. Despite the deep discounts, the great "deals," I was drowning in things I didn't need, or even want. And yet I wasn't quite sure how to *stop* wanting it either.

I began to crave and to seek a different sort of life for myself and for my family, one that wasn't defined by what we had but by *who we are*. I began a new quest for the Good Life.

Not Just about the Money

The insatiable desire for more is a disease that permeates every fiber of our being. Overconsumption and unchecked indulgence in *anything*—whether it is food, alcohol, drugs, or possessions—will eventually destroy us. Overspending and a desire to have *more* are addictions like any others, but ones that must be tempered in order for us to survive. *We must learn to control our love of money, or it will control us.*

Developing the discipline to control your spending, to consume less, to stick to a budget, and to save for the future is a habit that can't help but spill over into every other aspect of your life. Likewise, you can't live a truly productive, contented, and joy-filled life while your finances are in complete disarray. A Good Life and financial stability go hand in hand.

It doesn't matter if we are just barely squeaking by or we have more than we know what to do with, though most of us fall somewhere between those two extremes. Discovering the Good Life is not just about learning to spend less, but about actually changing the desires of our heart, shifting our priorities from wanting and hoping for the best of everything in this world to deeply longing to store up a different kind of treasure.

Remember those words of Paul: "But those who *desire* to be rich fall into temptation, into a snare, into many senseless and harmful desires that plunge people into ruin and destruction. For the love of money is a root of all kinds of evils. It is through this *craving* that some have wandered away from the faith and pierced themselves with many pangs."

But there is more to this chapter. There is a call to go down a different path:

> But you, man and woman of God, flee from all this, and pursue righteousness, godliness, faith, love, endurance and gentleness. Fight the good fight of the faith. Take hold of the eternal life to which you were called ...
>
> Do not be arrogant or put your hope in wealth,

which is so uncertain, but put your hope in God, who richly provides us with everything for our enjoyment. Do good, be rich in good deeds, and be generous and willing to share. In this way you will lay up treasure for yourself as a firm foundation for the coming age, *so that you may take hold of the life that is truly life.*

1 TIMOTHY 6:11–12, 17–19,
italics mine, some verses paraphrased

That, my friends, *is* the Good Life. Don't fall into the trap of defining the value of your life by what you have or by what you wish you had instead of by *who you are.* You may not fully realize it, but you are a child of a patient, loving, and forgiving Father. You are called to serve him and *only him,* and you are — whether or not you believe it — saved by an amazing, infallible, completely undeserved grace that doesn't care how big your house is, what you drive, or what you wear.

Praying for Change

My own transformation from a shopaholic to "money-saving expert" did not happen overnight, nor is it even close to being complete. I did not merely wake up one morning and declare, *Today I no longer care about the things of this world. Today I will stop shopping, stop longing, and stop trying to fill my life with things that don't satisfy.*

Oh, no.

While perhaps that is the experience of some people — perhaps even you — for me it has been a slow and often painful process. I have found that overturning a lifetime of consumption while the rest of the world still screams at me to keep wildly spending does not come without hard work, serious soul-searching, and lots and lots of intentional prayer. I have fervently and frequently prayed for God to change my heart, to lead me where *he* would have me go, and to *take away my desire for the things of this world*. I'm still praying that prayer.

It is a terrifying prayer because, quite frankly, I *love* the things of this world. I'm not eager to give up my nice house with its lovely decorations, granite countertops, and 600-thread-count sheets. Storing up treasures in heaven is all well and good, but I still want to drive a nice car, wear nice clothes, and continue Instagramming all my social-media-worthy moments on the latest version of the iPhone.

When I started praying that prayer, my less-than-noble goals included making enough money so I could fly first-class—or better yet, via private jet—rather than settling for coach. I wanted to be able to afford a full-time personal assistant to handle all the little day-to-day tasks I often dreaded. I desired a closet full of designer dresses, with cleverly coordinated accessories. I longed for a big house, a decorator to furnish it, and a live-in maid to clean it. I wanted the celebrity lifestyle I saw on television. I wanted to be rich. I wanted to *be* someone. I wanted to *make it*.

Ultimately the deep dissatisfaction I felt in my heart told me I was pursuing the wrong things. I already had so much and yet still felt empty. I longed to be full. But the accumulation of more stuff wasn't filling me. It left me empty. So I began to pray.

While I'd like to think this book can change your life, the reality is that *true* change will come only through prayer. The upcoming chapters of this book will contain more practical tips than you will probably know what to do with. We'll talk about choosing contentment, finding our sweet spots, setting goals, becoming more disciplined, clearing our lives of clutter, establishing a budget, saving money on food, keeping a clean house, and learning to appreciate all the things that money *can't* buy. I truly hope those ideas will help and encourage you to lead a simpler, happier, and more productive life. But I can tell you right now that nothing else in this book will mean anything without continual, wholehearted, and *passionate* prayer.

In Mark 11:24, Jesus told his disciples, "Therefore I tell you, whatever you ask for in prayer, believe that you have received it, and it will be yours." In Philippians 4:6–7, Paul writes, "Do not be anxious about anything, but in everything by prayer and petition, with thanksgiving, present your requests to God. And the peace of God, which transcends all understanding, will guard your hearts and your minds in Christ Jesus."

The Bible is very clear about this point: If we pray for God to change our heart, *God will answer*. Our hearts will change. Romans 12:2 reads, "Do not conform to the pattern of this world, *but be transformed by the renewing of your mind. Then you will be able to test and approve what God's will is*—his good, pleasing and perfect will" (emphasis mine).

The Good Life, Defined

Over the course of my years-long journey, as I continue to make this my daily prayer, my priorities and life goals have slowly begun to shift. I now long for a different type of richness, a richness that comes only from fullness in Christ.

As life has gone on, I've also realized that the old tagline of my blog, "The adventure of finding style and luxury on a budget," no longer fits my quest. It's not that I don't still enjoy great taste or a little splurge here and there—who doesn't, really?—but having a life full of nice things is no longer the endgame.

Instead, I want to find that Good Life defined so beautifully in the book of 1 Timothy. I want to pursue righteousness, godliness, faith, love, endurance, and gentleness. I want to fight the good fight of the faith. I want to take hold of the eternal life to which I was called. I do not want to be arrogant or put my hope in wealth, which is so uncertain, but to put my hope in God, who richly provides us with everything for our enjoyment. I want to do good, be rich in good deeds, and be generous and willing to share. In this way I will lay up treasure for myself as a firm foundation for the coming age, *so that I may take hold of the life that is truly life.*

The Good Life to me is this: a life rich in faith, family, friends, and creativity. It is a life full of the richness that God has to offer; a life spent building treasures in heaven rather than here on earth. It is not a life of laziness and greed, but one of discipline, hard work, and self-reflection. It may not always be easy or comfortable, but it is always full in abundance and completely secure in Christ.

That is the life I want to live. Care to join me?

CHALLENGE: **Define Your Good Life**

How do you think society's emphasis on wealth, success, and possessions affects you? Do you find yourself frequently longing for better and nicer things? Are your life goals and aspirations based on society's definition of success?

Identify any changes you need to make in your deepest heart's desires and motivations. Write them down and commit to spending time each day praying for transformation. God will change your heart; all you have to do is ask.

Contentment Is a Choice

Contentment makes poor men rich.
Discontentment makes rich men poor.

Benjamin Franklin

But godliness with contentment is
great gain. For we brought nothing into
the world, and we can take nothing out
of it. But if we have food and clothing,
we will be content with that.

1 Timothy 6:6 – 8

The greater part of our happiness or
misery depends on our dispositions
and not our circumstances.

Martha Washington

I can see it so clearly in my oldest daughter—that constant yearning and wanting and always needing something more. No sooner does she get what she wants than she is on to the next thing, constantly pining for something else that is just out of reach. She is seemingly incapable of simply enjoying the moment, of appreciating what she has instead of worrying about what she is missing out on. Her insatiable need for something more scares me sometimes.

And yet.

We are celebrating our anniversary at our favorite restaurant. It's an old-Florida-style place, steeped in tradition, with waiters in tuxedos, and white linen and fresh flowers on the tables, and where the seafood is flown in fresh daily and dining is an Event, not just an experience. Our food arrives, and I pick up my fork to try my pasta primavera. It's amazing, but I barely taste the delicately balanced flavors and signature lemon cream sauce because I'm already eyeing the dessert menu in front of me and dreaming of the warm Southern pecan praline tart I plan to order next. Then I spot my husband's choice—the herb-crusted, honey-grilled salmon. It looks incredible, fresh and perfectly flaky, and I can tell he is in heaven, relishing every bite. I wistfully eye his plate, hoping he'll share.

Why didn't I order that?

I open my closet and stand staring at my choices for a

full five minutes, disgusted and disheartened by what I see. *I've got nothing to wear*, I cry. *Everything in my closet is ugly!* My husband is unmoved and shoots me a look of exasperation that can only come from a man who has been down this road many, many times before. I try again. *Plus, it all makes me look fat!* He attempts to reason with me, which we both know is not going to end well, but he can't seem to help himself. *Didn't you just order two new pairs of jeans last week? And some new boots? And you just bought some new tops from Anthropologie a few weeks ago!* I know he's right, but I can't explain it.

What is it I'm still looking for?

I am covered in paint from my latest home decorating project, converting our guest-turned-junk-room to a far more functional family room. It is a surprise for my husband, who has been out of town on a business trip, and the last four days have been a nonstop flurry of planning and projects and procurement. There are new floors, new shelves, and new furniture, and a space that finally matches our vision. Still, I'm a wreck. Will he like it? Those surprise decorating shows make it look much more fun on TV. The girls and I wait nervously for Daddy to get home, and by the time we finally hear the door I am on pins and needles. I needn't have worried. "It's amazing," he says. "I absolutely love it!" He then points out something I hadn't considered. "Do you realize this means we've finally finished every room in the house?" I shake my head. *Oh no, there's still more to do. It can't be quite there yet.*

When will I be done?

I'm not feeling well, so I spend the morning in bed,

determined to take it easy and catch up on all my magazine reading. Cozily tucked under the covers, I am surrounded with three months' worth of all my favorites — *House Beautiful, Better Homes and Gardens, Martha Stewart Living, Real Simple,* and *Southern Living,* along with the latest issues of *People* and *US Weekly.* My mind starts turning as I am overloaded with ideas for improving my home and kitchen and menu and wardrobe. Suddenly I am filled with longing for a home that looks more put together and a gourmet kitchen filled with gadgets, where I do nothing but cook all day long. I read the latest Hollywood gossip and wonder why I can't be thinner or more beautiful or look picture-perfect arriving at LAX after a twelve-hour flight. So I put the magazines aside and instead begin scrolling on Facebook, where I see that one friend just remodeled her bathroom and another is now harvesting her own organic eggs from a designer chicken coop. This one is having another baby, while that one just posted photos from her recent vacation to Tahiti. She looks tanned and happy and skinny in her cute little bikini, and as I try hard not to hate her, all I feel is inadequate.

Why can't my life be more like that?

I'm supposed to be writing, but instead I spend the afternoon perusing my favorite blogs. This one's book just made the *New York Times* bestsellers list, while that one just hit 200,000 fans on Facebook. Another was recently featured on the *Today* show after her hilarious-but-insightful post on the trials of motherhood went viral. I begin to doubt my own self-worth as I compare their success with my own. I quickly forget that the past week has seen my own professional triumph; instead, the instant I reach one milestone, I'm already striving for the next. It is simply one more step on the road to ... well, where exactly I'm not sure. I tell myself I'll know it when I get there.

When will I know I've arrived?

Our children are so often an honest reflection of ourselves, and I know that the discontentment I recognize and fear in my daughter is fully present in my own day-to-day life. I far too often find myself getting caught in the pursuit of wanting something new, in the trap of thinking *there* is better than *here*, of telling myself the reason I'm not satisfied is that I don't have X or I haven't achieved Y. They are the familiar lies that keep creeping back over and over again.

I don't think I'm alone. These are the same lies we all must rebel against and actively fight back against. Defeating the lies is a conscious decision, one that requires daily effort and persistence and grace. This is a battle we have to win on purpose; we must *choose* contentment.

Easier said than done.

I have to admit that sometimes it feels like the world is just one big advertisement, conspiring to tell us we don't yet have whatever it is we need to be happy or successful. Between television, books, online media, magazines, billboards, and even the messages we get from our friends and family, it is practically impossible to escape the pressure to have more, do more, or be more. Much of that message involves filling our lives with things, promoting the idea that stuff will make us happy. Sometimes it is just a motivational message, simply telling us we should be better. In any case, the idea that what we have and who we are is enough is rarely—if ever—promoted. Contentment just doesn't sell.

So how do we *choose* contentment when it feels like life throws us nothing but ways to feel inadequate? How do we find fulfillment in what we have, when it is so painfully clear what we are still missing? How can we choose to be satisfied when the yearning for what we don't have feels so insatiable?

Knowing What Matters Most

The only real solution is to change the message to our brain. That starts by realizing our priorities. If we aren't perfectly clear about what is most important in our lives, it is easy to be swayed by anything that comes our way. Without a precise road map to guide us in knowing exactly what matters most of all, it is nearly impossible to combat the idea that something new is somehow better than what we already have.

What would happen if we took the time to actually write down our current priorities? How would our perspective change if we took just a few moments to determine what it is we want most out of life? Would our lists include having bigger houses, better clothes, nicer cars, or the latest tech gadgets? Do our highest aspirations really include having more *things*?

What would happen if we took it one step further and asked ourselves this question:

If I were to die tomorrow, what would people remember me for?

I don't know about you, but I sure don't want my friends and family to remember me for my killer shoe collection, or for my perfectly decorated house, or even for the great parties I used to throw or the delicious meals I used to cook. I certainly don't want them to look back on my life and think, *She was so self-absorbed.* Or, *She did nothing to help others.* Or, *Wow, she sure had a whole lot of stuff she didn't need.*

The Bible tells us to store up treasures in heaven, *for where our treasure is, there our heart will be also.* Remembering our end goal makes it a whole lot easier to set our priorities and determine what matters most. In fact, the Bible is pretty clear when it comes to letting us know what our priorities should be:

> But the fruit of the Spirit is love, joy, peace, patience, kindness, goodness, faithfulness, gentleness, self-control; against such things there is no law.
>
> GALATIANS 5:22–23 ESV

> Therefore, as God's chosen people, holy and dearly loved, clothe yourselves with compassion, kindness, humility, gentleness and patience. Bear with each other and forgive one another if any of you has a grievance against someone. Forgive as the Lord forgave you. And over all these virtues put on love, which binds them all together in perfect unity.
>
> COLOSSIANS 3:12–14

> Finally, brothers and sisters, whatever is true, whatever is noble, whatever is right, whatever is pure, whatever is lovely, whatever is admirable—if anything is excellent or praiseworthy—think about such things.
>
> PHILIPPIANS 4:8

> Love must be sincere. Hate what is evil; cling to what is good. Be devoted to one another in love. Honor one another above yourselves.
>
> ROMANS 12:9–10

Notice any recurring themes here? We are very clearly called to live a life of love and joy and peace. To practice kindness and patience, gentleness and self-control. To serve with compassion and humility. There's nothing there about having the best of everything, or about taking as much as we can get, or even about being in shape or beautiful or dressed to the nines.

It is so very easy to get entangled in the trap of wanting what we see around us. In fact, just a few minutes scrolling through Pinterest will reveal just how much we don't have. It takes real effort to actively long for the intangible and to truly want something we can't see or touch or feel. But when we really begin to look at our lives in terms of eternity — even if for just a few minutes — instead of what we want *right now*, having a designer wardrobe or a bigger house or a prettier kitchen suddenly doesn't seem quite so important.

Taming the Green-Eyed Monster

Of course setting our priorities is only step one. The reality of being human is that even if we know what we *should* be aiming for, we will still continually be swayed by the temptations of everyday life. No matter how much we have, it is easy to see what someone else does or is or has and suddenly want that for ourselves. That green-eyed monster lives within all of us.

As a writer, I am constantly tempted to compare myself to others in my field. I'll see another author doing well and think, *Why are they so much better than me?* I'll read a thought-provoking or insightful article and wonder, *Why can't I think of that?* But I don't stop there. I begin questioning everything I am doing, second-guessing my own path, my own content, my own self-worth. Suddenly everything I write is garbage and I might as well quit altogether.

Your temptation to compare might look different than mine, but chances are it leaves you feeling just as inadequate. Perhaps it is the other women in your Bible study. They all seem so on top of things. They always read the entire book right on schedule and come prepared with a whole list of thought-provoking questions and intelligent insights. You, on the other hand, usually only end up finding time to read the first two or three chapters, instead relying on the detailed book reviews you find on Amazon.com to have even the faintest understanding of the theme. Most of the evening is spent frantically praying that no one bothers to ask your opinion, and every month you wonder why you can't seem to pull yourself together.

Or maybe you find yourself envying the seemingly charmed life of your older sister. She used to be so sweet, so *normal*, and now every time the two of you meet for coffee she has something new to brag about, whether it be that her husband just made partner, her surprise weekend trip to New York City, her new Audi, or the sparkling 2-carat diamond on her finger. You try very hard not to roll your eyes as she chatters endlessly about the difficulty of finding a nanny and the latest country club drama, and it takes every ounce of willpower you can muster not to yell, *These are not real problems!* And yet you can't help but wish you had just a little of what she had.

Maybe it's the other moms in your circle of friends who have you feeling like you don't quite measure up. One has the patience of a saint and never utters an unkind word about anyone. Her whole face lights up around her children as she happily sits on the floor playing with Legos like it was the most interesting thing in the world. You wish you could somehow capture just a little of her enthusiasm. Another runs five miles every morning, eats nothing but salads, and has the perfect body to show for it. Her stylish clothes and short skirts show off her long legs and lean muscles. You wish you had the time or energy to put into looking that good. Yet another is on the fast track to success, having just been promoted for the third time this year. She seems so genuinely happy and excited about her work, and after every conversation you find yourself longing for a career you truly love.

No matter where dissatisfaction strikes or we don't feel we measure up, that green-eyed monster will destroy us if we let it. True contentment will never be found by looking outward. If we struggle with wanting the things we see around us, we need to *stop looking*. We should stop reading blogs and magazines or watching television shows that make us feel inadequate. If our struggle is with certain people in our lives who bring that insecurity, that longing, that monster right to the surface, we might consider taking a break, at least until we've managed to quiet the discontent in our own hearts.

The important thing to remember is that another person's success or talent doesn't negate our own. Likewise, another person's wealth doesn't make our lives any less valuable. Romans 12:6 tells us that "we have different gifts, according to the grace given to each of us." No two people will walk the exact same path, and *nothing someone else has will fulfill us if we are not already filled.* Our only job is to keep our eyes on our own path, then walk it to the very best of our ability.

An Attitude of Gratitude

Discontentment can sneak up on us so quickly, often before we even realize it is happening. Something doesn't go exactly our way, and suddenly we are wishing the whole world was different. I especially see this in my kids, who can be perfectly satisfied one minute, then begging for something new the next. I have found that it helps both them and me to have daily conversations about the blessings in our lives and the things we are grateful for. We call it our Attitude of Gratitude.

Philippians 4:4, 6−7 reminds us to "rejoice in the Lord always. I will say it again: Rejoice!... Do not be anxious about anything, but in every situation, by prayer and petition, with thanksgiving, present your requests to God. And the peace of God, which transcends all understanding, will guard your hearts and your minds in Christ Jesus."

It is easy to bring our concerns and requests before God. Sometimes we treat prayer like a fast-food restaurant, barking out our order so we can get in and out and be done. *Uh, yeah, okay, God ... I'll take some grace, blessings, and a double side of patience today. Oh, and why don't you throw in some healing for good measure.*

We forget—or at least I do—that we must also be intentional about thanking God for what he has done in our lives and in the lives of others. Taking the time to consciously list all the specific ways in which we have been blessed can't but help our perspective. An attitude of continual gratitude is the fastest way to chase away that green-eyed beast.

Of course, if you are really struggling with feelings of discontentment, you may not be feeling very blessed. You may have no idea of where to even start.

If so, consider that:

- **You are reading this book.** According to UNESCO, 26 percent of the world's adult population is illiterate, and women make up two-thirds of that number. There is a strong correlation between the poorest countries and those with the lowest literacy rate. Moreover, people in many countries around the world, including China, Iran, Syria, Saudi Arabia, Vietnam, and North Korea, have tightly restricted access to books, newspapers, and the Internet.[1] *Reading is a gift.*

- **You are not hungry.** In the past twenty-four hours, you've probably eaten at least three full meals, and chances are you've never had to experience the pain or exhaustion caused by lack of food, or the fear of not knowing where your next meal will come from. The United Nations Food and Agriculture Organization estimates that 870 million people, or roughly one-eighth of the world's population, are suffering from chronic hunger. In fact, one-third of children in developing countries are considered malnourished, and more than one-half of the deaths of children each year are linked to poor nutrition.[2] *Food is a gift.*

- **You have access to medicine.** As the debate over health care rages in Washington and lines are drawn in the sand, we sometimes forget how fortunate we are to even be having such a debate. We don't think twice about the antibiotics, vaccines, painkillers, and prenatal care that keep us healthy. And yet the World Health Organization estimates that between 1.3 and 2.1 billion people in the world do not have access to even the most basic medicines. The WHO also reports that this lack of medical access is strongly correlated to decreased life expectancy.[3] *Access to quality health care is a gift.*

- **You can drive.** It might not be that brand-new Audi you've been dreaming of. It might even be dirty and dented and way past its prime, but if you own your own vehicle, you are in the lucky 9 percent of the world's population that does.[4] *Transportation is a gift.*

- **You have a place to sleep tonight.** Chances are you've even got your very own bed—with sheets, blankets, and a pillow to go with it. According to the UN Commission on Human Rights, there are an estimated 100 million people without homes around the world, including between 600,000 and 2.5 million homeless right here in the United States.[5] Even scarier, one in three Americans is only one paycheck away from being homeless.[6] *A place to call home is a gift.*

- **You can turn on the lights.** It is sometimes hard to feel grateful when faced with a $100+ electric bill, but most of us would need to spend only a day or two without electricity to be cured of ever complaining again. But believe it or not, more than 1.2 *billion* people in the world still don't have access to electricity.[7] *Electricity is a gift.*

- **You are not thirsty.** How many times a day do we drink a glass of water or use the toilet or wash our hands without once stopping to think of where that water came from, or where it might go next? But the scary truth is that 780 million people in the world lack access to clean water. Even more sobering is the fact that every year 3.4 million people, many of them children, *die* from water-related diseases.[8] *Clean water is a gift.*

There is a strange magic that happens the minute we stop comparing our lives to those we perceive as having more, and instead begin intentionally appreciating all that we really have. We just tend to take all that basic, boring stuff for granted, but chances are we have all been blessed with gifts that many people don't have. When we open our hearts just enough to see the blessings we've already been given, our whole worldview changes from one of longing to one of overwhelming gratitude and joy.

Turning Insecurity Inside Out

Of course, that gratitude and joy are often fleeting and so easily replaced by feelings of self-doubt. One minute we are fine, the next minute a ball of insecurity. And quite honestly, I don't think the battle to choose contentment in the midst of inadequacy ever really goes away. One minute we're doing great, and the next we are in way over our heads, caught in a pit where it feels like everyone else is smarter or better or more successful.

I traveled to a conference not long ago, one where I knew I wasn't going to know anyone ahead of time. I am secretly terrified of these types of social settings, the ones that require me to "put myself out there" and act extroverted and friendly when in reality I want nothing more than to hide away in my hotel room. It did not begin well. As the first day progressed and I started comparing myself to all the other far more successful people in the room, it was all I could do not to shrivel up in a ball of self-doubt.

Finally, toward the end of the day, I spotted across the room the friend of a friend, a woman I didn't know personally but someone I knew *of*. I figured she might become an ally in this sea of people who were clearly better than me. She was busy talking, so I sat at my table for at least fifteen minutes, trying to work up the courage to say hello. Finally, I took a deep breath, walked across the room, and haltingly, awkwardly, and painfully introduced myself.

She did not welcome me with open arms. While I realize now that my own insecurities may have skewed my perception of the situation, in that moment I felt nothing but the crushing weight of rejection and the humiliation of trying to befriend a girl who had no interest in returning the favor. I couldn't escape fast enough, and when I finally made it back to my room, I collapsed on the bed and cried myself to sleep.

Had it even remotely been an option, I would've most certainly been on the next flight home, but alas, I was stuck. The next morning, my friend Edie called to check in, knowing just how nervous I had been about the trip. "How's it going, honey?" she asked gently. "Are you learning anything yet?" Trying not to cry again, I told her that coming to the conference had been a huge mistake. "I'm such a loser," I said. "What am I even doing here? I'm just not good enough for this."

While she was sympathetic to my plight, she refused to let me wallow in self-pity. Instead, she gently told me I was approaching the whole situation all wrong. "You're only thinking of yourself," she said, "when you need to be looking at what you have to offer to others." She then pointed out that while there were certainly people at that conference who were a whole lot more successful than me, there were just as many people who were feeling insecure. "Don't worry about how uncomfortable you feel," she said. "Instead, just find someone you can bless today."

I knew she was exactly right, so I put on my big-girl pants and went back down to the conference, determined to find a way to bless someone else. As it turned out, the opportunities to mentor and encourage others were all around me. I realized again that it is so easy in those situations to let our insecurities get the best of us. Because we are feeling weak, we turn inward, focusing on our own doubts and fears while wishing that others would reach out and provide the validation or encouragement we are so desperate to hear. But this is totally the wrong approach. Focusing on our own inadequacy only feeds the flame. Instead, contentment comes when we are able to make the conscious choice to turn our insecurities inside out, to focus on what we have to offer others rather than on how they can serve us.

Eliminating Temptation

Sometimes finding contentment is as simple as choosing to steer clear of the things that cause us to stumble. It means staying away from all those things that make us feel unworthy or like we just don't have enough. For me, it was making a conscious decision to avoid Target and the mall, and to unsubscribe to emails and catalogs from my favorite stores. It meant not reading certain blogs or magazines, or watching certain television shows (like anything on HGTV). For a while it even meant spending less time with friends.

Not surprisingly, it is this particular aspect of choosing contentment that has helped the most in my battle to spend less. Avoiding the temptation to *want* more things also means avoiding the temptation to *buy* more things. It's really a win-win.

A life of true contentment is one we have to work for, and one we have to actively *choose*. It means taking the time to identify our priorities and to know what truly matters in life. It means being intentional about desiring the things we can't see rather than all that glitters around us. It means making the decision to stop looking at what everyone else has, but instead working to tame those ever-present comparison and envy inclinations that bubble just below the surface. It means adopting an attitude of gratitude for all we've already been given and being willing to turn our insecurities inside out. Finally, it means actively eliminating those things that tempt us the most.

Are you ready to make the choice?

CHALLENGE: Choose Contentment

Spend a few minutes thinking about your priorities. What are the things that are most important to you? What kind of person do you want to be? Then take it one step further. If you were to die tomorrow, what would you want people to remember you for?

Next think about the people you most often compare yourself to. What is it about their lives that makes you feel envious or inadequate? Would your life really be different if you had what they had? Now think about all the blessings and gifts you do have. Write them down and spend some time in prayer, thanking God for all he's given you.

Finally, think about where you can actively eliminate temptation in your life. What stores can you stay out of? What magazines, television shows, or websites can you turn off or avoid? Develop a concrete plan for keeping temptation at bay.

We All Have a Sweet Spot

People are most successful when they are in their sweet spot. Your sweet spot is the intersection where your passion meets your greatest strength.

Ken Coleman

We have different gifts, according to the grace given to each of us. If your gift is prophesying, then prophesy in accordance with your faith; if it is serving, then serve; if it is teaching, then teach; if it is to encourage, then give encouragement; if it is giving, then give generously; if it is to lead, do it diligently; if it is to show mercy, do it cheerfully.

Romans 12:6 – 8

My friend Alysha owns and operates her own wildly successful salon and boutique in downtown Bellingham, Washington. It is a darling little shop, sleek and stylish and full of sparkle. It is appropriately named *Bliss*, and simply walking through the door makes you feel a little more glamorous, a little prettier, just a little more special. Her chic display racks are filled with carefully curated tops and skirts and dresses, each piece individually selected by Alysha's expert eye. Whether she is styling their hair or styling their wardrobe, she has a way of making everyone who walks through her door feel absolutely beautiful and one of a kind. She is not just *good* at what she does; she is *great*.

Alysha and I have been best friends since the sixth grade. I consider her one of my oldest and dearest friends, and as such, I have had a front-row seat to all the times she was underestimated by the people around us. While I did very little actual work in high school, instead skating by on my reputation as an "A" student, Alysha studied hard. Though she worked much more diligently, she was labeled an "average" student and earned mostly C's. She didn't play sports, wasn't involved in clubs or drama, was never voted into student council, and had no interest in the yearbook or school newspaper. She never really stood out or commanded attention. To many people she was simply ordinary. Nothing special. Forgettable.

But those people didn't know Alysha like I did. They didn't see her quiet drive and determination. They didn't see how she worked her way through high school, saving enough money to pay for community college and beauty school while everyone else was involved in lots of activities. They didn't see how the personal tragedies in her life—first losing her dad as a child and then her brother in her early twenties—only inspired her to work that much harder to achieve her dreams because she understood all too well that life is short and precious. They didn't see how she consistently pushed herself to be better, becoming an expert in her field and learning everything she could, not just about doing hair, but about fashion and style and running a successful business. They didn't see how even when things went horribly wrong, she kept doing what she loved.

Although we now live more than three thousand miles apart, Alysha still inspires me every day. She is the epitome of someone who has followed her dreams despite all odds, and she was very clearly *born* to do what she is doing. While I'm sure it hurt deeply to be written off by some as "average," she never let that judgment stand in her way, and she even managed to avoid becoming bitter, though bitterness would have been an easy path. She followed her passion, figured out what she loved doing most of all—what she was made to do—and never looked back.

How many of us can say we've been that brave?

Finding Your Sweet Spot

Where is *your* passion? What do *you* love doing most of all? What activity makes you jump out of bed in the morning, or rush home from work just so you can have a little more time for it? If you could do only one thing right now, what would it be? Would it be sewing? Styling hair or running your own boutique like Alysha? Would it be crafting or scrapbooking? Running marathons? Speaking or leading a Bible study? Volunteering? Teaching? Starting your own home-based business? Learning a trade? Becoming healthy after an illness or depression? Going back to school? Raising children or spending more time with your grandchildren? Becoming a missionary? Mentoring other women?

For me, it is writing. On some level, it has always been writing. For as long as I can remember, I loved writing and dreamed of becoming a writer, even though another—often much louder—voice told me it was a silly dream. I had no idea *what* I wanted to write; I just knew that the process of putting pen to paper was for me as essential as breathing.

Our sweet spot is that place where our greatest passions and our talents or abilities intersect. It is that special place where we are able to do whatever it is that we feel *most* called to do, that thing we *love*, that thing we are *great* at, that thing that makes life worth living. Living in the sweet spot means having the courage to follow our dreams, take risks, and work harder than we ever thought possible in order to accomplish our goals. It means refusing to be bogged down by the monotony of the everyday, even if that drudgery occupies 99 percent of our time.

Living in our sweet spot means not only taking the time to discover our passions and to realize what it is we were made to do, but also being willing to take the next step. It is not enough to know in theory what we'd like to do; we also have to *do it*. We have to do it with abandon, do it in every spare moment we can find, do it as if our life depends on it, regardless of the circumstances and regardless of whether the timing is just right.

I think most of us have the tendency to put our dreams on hold in favor of the practical. I certainly did. We put our passion on the back burner, telling ourselves we'll get to it someday, when the kids are older and things aren't quite so crazy. Perhaps after the mortgage has been paid off and we're a little more financially secure, *then* we'll be ready. We convince ourselves that we can't do it right now because there are just *so many other things* that need to be done first.

The hard truth is that following our passion and living out our dreams is incredibly scary. There is a huge potential for failure. It makes us vulnerable to criticism from people who don't understand. It gives others an opportunity to laugh at us or cut us down. It means taking a step into the unknown, where anything can happen, and where we don't always have control. After all, it is much easier to find shelter in the known than risk the heartbreak of having it all come crashing down.

I know how scary it is because I have been there. I put my own dreams of writing on hold for many years, choosing instead to pursue a totally different career path. It wasn't until I started blogging—mostly on a whim—in 2010 that I even remembered how much I loved to write. That one small step ignited the passion that had always been burning inside of me. And this time I wouldn't let it go. I began writing and didn't stop, even when no one around me understood it, even when my husband questioned me, and even when my friends made fun of me behind my back. There were more than a few times when I felt like quitting, and it took *years* before anyone actually began reading—and responding to—what I was writing.

But you know what? Even if not a *single person* ever read another word I wrote, *I would keep writing.* Just like Alysha knows she was born to make women look and feel beautiful, I know now that I was born to do *this* work. Writing is fully my passion. I think living well, at its very core, is finding that sweet spot, and my life is full because I am right in the place I need to be.

Bloom Where You Are

There are times, however, when we have no idea what our sweet spot is or how to find it. Furthermore, as our season of life changes and evolves, our dreams, aspirations, and callings can too. Every now and then we discover that what once ignited our passions no longer interests us. Sometimes it takes being unhappy or dissatisfied—discontented even— with something in our lives to spur us to make a change. Sometimes seeing what someone else is doing makes us see what we truly want or need to do. And sometimes we have to realize that even when we aren't living in our sweet spot, we are still called to make the most of the circumstances we are in.

There is a big difference between wanting what we don't have just for the sake of wanting more and wanting to do something else because we know, deep down, it is where we are meant to be. It is often difficult to strike a balance between a healthy longing for something more and choosing peace, no matter our circumstances. After all, how are we supposed to find our sweet spot when we are stuck in a job or a town or a situation we don't love? How do we remedy the tension between choosing contentment and striving for more?

My sister has a term for it. She tells me to *bloom where you are.*

The first time she said this to me was just after my first daughter was born. My husband had begun working for a company on the other side of the state, about three and a half hours from our house. While we were happy he had found a job at all — aerospace engineering jobs were not that easy to come by in Florida — we weren't exactly thrilled about our options. It was too far to commute, so Chuck could either stay in a cheap motel all week and come home just on the weekends, or we could try to find something to rent. West Palm Beach isn't exactly known for its affordable housing options, so we rented a tiny one-bedroom apartment that we not so lovingly referred to as "The Box."

I hated The Box.

Because we were sharing a car, most days I was stuck in The Box with a colicky newborn for ten to twelve hours a day. I was bored and lonely and altogether miserable, and my sister's advice was to bloom where you are!

It took a while for those words to sink in. I wish I could

say I learned to embrace The Box and that we made the most of it, but that's not what happened. We ultimately realized our sanity was on the line. Chuck got a new job three thousand miles away, in Washington State, and we proceeded to move seven more times over the next three years.

But her words stuck with me, and with every move I found them ringing a little truer. "Bloom where you are" became my mantra, and the more I took it to heart, the more I was willing to see the opportunities lying right in front of me. In Tacoma, while working as a spa director, I organized an annual charity fashion show called *Biella for the Cure* that raised thousands of dollars for breast cancer research. In Everett, as a stay-at-home mom, I founded a mom's group called BoMoToGoMo (Boeing Moms of Tots Who Want to Get Out More) that is still active to this day. And then, in 2010, I started a silly little blog about my own adventure of living well and spending less that has since grown to become one of the most popular personal finance blogs on the Internet, reaching more than a million readers each month.

At any given time, we *all* have room to grow and bloom, no matter where we are planted. No matter our season of life, we each have opportunities to learn more, develop more, give more. A young working wife may watch her sister become a mother, feel the stirrings of envy, and realize that she, too, may someday want to nurture and tend a family. On the other hand, the stay-at-home mom whose children are now grown may wistfully look at the success of her career-minded college roommate and be inspired to run for public office or finally go back to school to get her master's degree. Our sweet spot doesn't even have to be some grand life plan;

on the contrary, sometimes we don't even know what our sweet spot is but simply need to follow our current calling or passion. That calling may be as simple as finding the time to be creative or learning how to cook, or even figuring out how to use coupons to save money and get out of debt.

Finding our sweet spot means listening to that tiny voice inside of us that says, *Make the most of where you are right now. Learn. Grow. Develop who and what you are.* And often the sweet spot will emerge, right in the middle of living life.

Identifying Our Gifts

We are often our own worst critics, so prone to easily picking out all the things we are *not* good at, while failing to recognize the areas in which we shine. But trust me when I tell you that we *all* have been given our own special gifts and talents. In fact, I am pretty sure we all have at least a *few* things we do very well, even if those skills may not seem important or special or even very useful sometimes.

Your gift may be leadership or wisdom or discernment or patience. It could be kindness or administration or communication or diligence. It may be generosity or healing or knowledge or empathy. Perhaps it is teaching or organization or creativity or music. Maybe it is even just *doing* or serving or being able to step up when needed. We are all blessed with any number of special gifts and abilities. Some of us excel in forging a path for others, leading the way and administering change, while others are able to effectively serve in the background, quietly creating, organizing, or following through. And while some gifts may be flashier than others, or seem preferable or more important, they are *all* essential.

The truth is that all gifts come from God, in order to serve and glorify him: "There are different kinds of gifts, but the same Spirit distributes them. There are different kinds of service, but the same Lord. There are different kinds of working, but in all of them and in everyone it is the same God at work" (1 Corinthians 12:4–6). That same chapter goes on to explain that we are all a part of the body of Christ and that we are made up of many parts that work together:

> Even so the body is not made up of one part but of many. Now if the foot should say, "Because I am not a hand, I do not belong to the body," it would not for that reason stop being part of the body. And if the ear should say, "Because I am not an eye, I do not belong to the body," it would not for that reason stop being part of the body. If the whole body were an eye, where would the sense of hearing be? If the whole body were an ear, where would the sense of smell be? But in fact God has placed the parts in the body, every one of them, *just as he wanted them to be.*
>
> 1 CORINTHIANS 12:14–18, emphasis mine

Finding your sweet spot often involves a messy process of *finding* and then *learning* to embrace the God-given talents and aptitudes you already have rather than the ones you only wish you had. It means taking the time to discover what you are truly good at and enjoy, then figuring out how to merge that talent and those abilities with the ideas and dreams and pursuits you are most passionate about. And sometimes finding your sweet spot even means taking a wrong turn — and failing.

Choosing the Wrong Path

When I was a little girl, my dad told me I should be a lawyer. It was nothing more than an off-the-cuff remark, but from that moment on, I determined I was going to law school. As a kid I would watch *Matlock* obsessively and then pretend I was the one who proved the case and caused the star witness to crumble and confess on the stand. In high school I was required to research a career. Naturally, I chose law. I interviewed local lawyers, spent hours reading every book I could find, and sent away for applications to all the Ivy League law schools. The applications didn't really help my research paper, but I distinctly remember holing up in my room and drooling over the stately brick buildings and impressive law libraries, thinking, *Someday I'll be there too.*

In college I studied political science because it was the major that all the other pre-law students were taking, and I earned straight A's because I knew I'd need them if I wanted to get into a good law program. Those dreams were put on hold when I fell into a two-year-long bout with severe clinical depression. But even during the darkest days of my depression, the allure of going to law school never really faded. I'd lie in bed watching *Legally Blonde* over and over, and during my stay at the McLean psychiatric hospital in the Boston area, I used to spend my Saturdays wandering around Harvard Square pretending I was a student there too. When I finally recovered, I threw myself back into my studies. For the next two years I worked hard to finish my degree and study for the LSAT. At long last, I began applying to schools. My dream was finally within reach.

In the fall of 2004, I started law school at Washington University in Saint Louis. While the impressive campus was exactly what I had always envisioned, law school was nothing like I thought it would be. It was painfully dull and extremely tedious and fiercely competitive. I thought I was type A until I went to law school and realized my own ambition was *nothing* compared to the people I was going to law school with. Friends, let me tell you, there is a *reason* lawyers have such a cutthroat reputation!

Three-quarters of the way into my first year of law school, I was absolutely miserable. It took monumental effort just to get out of bed in the morning and to force myself to sit in boring, uninteresting class after tediously mind-numbing class. I couldn't believe that this dream I had pursued for so long was so awful, and so very different from what I thought it would be. I had never felt more stuck.

Then one Sunday afternoon, Chuck and I took a walk in the park near our house. As we walked, I rambled on about how much I hated school and how unhappy I was, how I couldn't stand the other students, and how excruciatingly dull it felt to sit in class all day long. He mostly just listened, without having much to say in return. Then suddenly he stopped dead in his tracks. He grabbed my shoulders and turned me to face him, looked me straight in the eye, and said, "You know you don't have to finish this, right? It's okay to quit."

Until that very second, quitting had never even occurred

to me. It simply wasn't an option. I had worked so hard to get there. I had quit my job. And Chuck had quit his job to come with me! We had moved halfway across the country and even *bought a house* in a city that we had no interest in. I had taken out massive student loans to pay for it all. Even with a few scholarships, law school was *expensive*. In my mind, there were no other options but to finish what I had started, even to the bitter end.

After all, if I quit, *who would I be?* This plan was all I knew.

But there he was, telling me it was okay. His permission to fail gave me just enough courage to walk into the dean of students' office the next morning to tell her I was leaving. She said something I will never forget. She said, "Normally I would try to talk a student out of something like this, but this is the first time I have seen you look genuinely happy all semester. You are doing the right thing."

It was an expensive but invaluable lesson, and one I have never forgotten.

Sometimes it is okay to fail.

I think sometimes we become so fearful of making a mistake, of doing something wrong, of having someone else laugh at us, that we become paralyzed with indecision. I thought quitting law school would be the end of the world, but it wasn't. Instead, the experience forever changed me. It taught me that failure is almost never fatal, and that life does go on and sometimes you just have to put one foot in front of the other until the new path becomes clear. But even more importantly, quitting law school opened doors to a whole world of possibilities, and the bold act of quitting gave me the bravery to try things I would never have considered before. Eventually I was able to find my sweet spot, not *despite* my failure, but *because* of it.

Jumping In with Both Feet

Both my daughters love to swim, but their approach to getting into the cold water couldn't be more different. Maggie, my oldest, is full of caution, carefully dipping just her toe at first to test the water, then slowly and painfully creeping in until the water is up to her neck. The process seems to take forever, and sometimes she gives up before she even makes it all the way in. Her little sister Annie, on the other hand, is always fully immersed in just seconds. Before she can give it a second thought, she'll happily take a running leap off the side and jump into the deep end with a satisfying splash. While the chill of the water may take her breath away for a second, she is always acclimated in almost no time at all. In fact, occasionally by the time her sister is *finally* ready to swim, Annie is already asking to get out.

When it comes to following our dreams and finding our sweet spot, I think many of us prefer to take Maggie's cautious approach. We try to get away with dipping just our toes in the water, wishing it weren't quite so cold and scary, when instead we could be jumping in with both feet. Taking that leap of faith is all at once the most terrifying and the most rewarding thing you may ever do.

My friend Alysha discovered this when she finally took the plunge and realized her dream of opening her own salon. She found out that being a business owner is hard. She suffered setbacks and disappointments, and was even betrayed by her business partner. More than a few times she wasn't sure she would make it, and there were many times when she felt like giving up. But she didn't. She knew she had found her sweet spot, and so she kept going, pursuing the path she was made for.

You may not know quite what your sweet spot is yet, and you may be worried you aren't quite good enough or you aren't smart or organized or talented enough, but I dare to bet that you are. Your passion may not be writing or opening your own boutique, but chances are it is something just as great, just as meaningful, and just as important. It can be awfully scary to jump into the unknown and pursue a dream you don't know will ever come true, but I can tell you from experience — it is the most exhilarating jump you will ever take.

My friends, I'm quite sure you all have a sweet spot too. My hope and prayer for you is that you will become fearless in all that you do, and you'll dare to take the plunge, even when it means risking failure. Remember those words of Philippians 4:13 (NKJV): "I can do all things through Christ who strengthens me." Don't let the possibility of falling short deter you from trying. Don't let the naysayers or that little voice in the back of your head prevent you from taking action. Don't let the messiness or trial-and-error nature of the process deter you. You *will* make mistakes. You *will* screw up along the way. There may even be times when you have to admit defeat. Keep going. Use those lessons as opportunities to discover what doesn't work, and always persevere.

CHALLENGE: **Identify Your Sweet Spot**

Spend some time thinking about your dreams and passions. What is it that you love to do most of all? What makes you jump out of bed in the morning, or rush home from work just so you can have a little more time for it? If you could do only one thing right now, what would it be? Is there something you've always wanted to do but haven't quite gathered the nerve to try?

Next spend some time listening to the whispers of holy discontentment in your life. Is there something in your life that isn't quite right? Do you have a feeling you are on the wrong path? What would it take to make a change?

Finally, consider your own gifts and talents. What are your areas of expertise? What are you good at? What do you most enjoy? What is your sweet spot?

Ignite that spark within you and give yourself permission to try, to leap in with both feet, even if it means risking failure.

Written Goals Can Change Your Life

First say to yourself what you would be, then do what you have to do.

Epictetus

But one thing I do: Forgetting what Is behind and straining toward what is ahead, I press on toward the goal to win the prize for which God has called me heavenward in Christ Jesus.

Philippians 3:13 – 14

Goals that are not written down are just wishes.

Anonymous

*A*fter three years of balancing stay-at-home-motherhood with building my own business, my daily routine was pretty well established. I started early — usually around 4:00 a.m. — so I could get at least four or five uninterrupted hours of work in before the kids woke up. I am at my best in the morning, so those quiet, predawn hours were always the most productive. The rest of the morning was spent tidying the house and then homeschooling. After a late lunch, the girls would settle in their room for a quiet time, and I would sneak in another hour or two of work before starting dinner or rushing off to all those afternoon activities. Every day was jam-packed, and I was often exhausted, but the routine was set — and it was *mine*.

And then my husband left his job to become a stay-at-home dad so I could pursue a full-time blogging and writing career. Suddenly my carefully regimented routine was turned upside down. Having him at home was a major goal we had been working toward for years, one we had talked about at length beforehand, and a change we really, truly wanted to make for our family. I thought I was prepared. I thought I was ready.

I was so *not* ready.

The reality of having Chuck home and in *my* space all the time was so much harder than I had ever imagined. For months I just felt "off." I would try to wake up early, but then he would wake up too. I would sit at my desk to work, but almost instantly get distracted. Sometimes it was the noise around me; other times it was email or Pinterest or the latest status updates on Facebook. I began spending an inordinate amount of time glued to my laptop or phone, but I wasn't *really* accomplishing anything. To make matters worse, the more time I spent "working," the more frustrated my husband became. "You're always on the computer," he would say. "You're here, but you're not present. We need you to engage."

Though I didn't want to admit it, I knew, deep down, he was right. My life was out of whack. I lacked a clear direction and focus, and as a result I was wasting far too much time on the things that didn't matter at all, and not finding any time for the things that did. Something had to give.

Filling the Time Jar

It wasn't the first time in my life I'd devolved from competent go-getter to utter disaster, seemingly overnight. Unfortunately, I'm pretty sure it won't be the last. I think we all suffer from these "slumps" once in a while, those days or weeks or months when we feel completely overwhelmed and hopelessly unproductive. We all have those moments when it feels like *no matter what we do*, we simply can't pull ourselves together or get caught up. The treadmill is moving just a little too fast, and there are one—or ten—too many things pulling us in all directions. The demands and stresses of the everyday become just a bit too much to bear, so we start looking for a way to escape. We respond by getting distracted, wasting time, and putting off doing the things that are most important. This, of course, creates a vicious cycle, because the more we procrastinate and allow ourselves to be distracted, the more behind we get, and the more overwhelmed we feel.

Perhaps you are even feeling like this right now.

There is a famous story about a professor who held up a jar of rocks to his students. He asked them, "Is this jar full?" They all agreed it was. Then he took out a bag of small pebbles and poured it into the jar. The pebbles filled the space around the rocks in the jar, and he asked, "*Now* is it full?" Everyone once again said yes. Next he took out a bag of sand and poured it into the jar. The sand filtered through the rocks and pebbles until all the spaces were filled. "What about now?" he asked. "Do you think it is full?" For the third time, the class said yes. Finally he took a pitcher of water and poured it into the jar until the water reached the brim and began spilling over the top. "Now," he said, "we can say this jar is really full." He then asked his class an important question: "Do you think if I had started with the water, then the sand, and then the pebbles, there would still have been room for the rocks?"

I love that story. I even keep a jar of rocks in my kitchen as a daily reminder that the jar represents life. We have to fill it with the big things first, because if we start with the little things—the water and sand and pebbles—there will be no room for the things that matter most. The rocks—our goals—are the difference between living life to the fullest and just getting by. Thus, if we want to live the Good Life, *we must fill our jar well*.

Creating a Long-Term Vision

In my early twenties I went through a devastating period of clinical depression. There really aren't a lot of good things to say about depression, but for me the scariest thing of all was feeling like I was living in a black hole of despair. The hopelessness was so all-encompassing that I simply couldn't imagine feeling any different than the way I was feeling right then. In the midst of it all, I just didn't believe — I just *couldn't* believe — that things would ever get better or that I would ever be well. I had no future, only darkness.

It was during this very dark time that my therapist encouraged me to write down some long-term goals. "Think about your life five or ten years from now," she said. "Where do you want to be?" She proceeded to ask me a series of questions, just to get me thinking: *Where do you live? What do you look like? Who are your friends? What do you do for work? What do you do for fun? Where do you go on vacation? Are you married? Do you have children? What have you accomplished? What does your home look like?*

At first I resisted. "This is stupid," I said. "In ten years I'll probably be dead anyway. What's the point?" But she persisted. "Just try it," she pleaded gently. "You might surprise yourself." Amazingly enough, as impossible as it was for me to believe that life would ever be different than the misery I was mired in right in that moment, it actually *wasn't* that difficult to imagine an ideal life ten years down the road. It was far enough away to not feel overwhelming. After all, ten years is a *long* time. Anything could happen in ten years.

Even a loser like me *might* be able to turn things around in ten years.

And so I made a list. I called it "What I Want My Life to Be Like 10 Years from Now." It included everything from the important, like *I want to be married to the love of my life* and *I want to be successfully pursuing a career that I love,* to the not quite so important, like *I want to have long hair* and *I want to learn how to garden.*

I wish I could say this was the turning point in my battle with depression. I'd love to tell you that making that list was the pivotal moment in which I suddenly realized life was worth living. It wasn't quite that simple. In fact, for a while I even got worse. Much worse. But I can say that in that moment a seed of hope was planted. If only for a moment, I was able to see a very small light at the end of a very long, very dark tunnel. It took a long time, but eventually I was able to accept the possibility that things could be different, that this vision of the future might actually be attainable if I was willing to take the first step.

I'm sure each of us can think of at least one super-successful, ultra-driven, goal-oriented person in our life. You know the type. She is the one who throws out well-worn clichés like, "All you need to do to be successful is set some goals" or "Shoot for the moon and even if you miss, you'll land among the stars." She seems to have no problem figuring out just what her goals should be and the precise number of action steps it will take to get there. It's almost like she's discovered some secret road map to life that the rest of us can only dream of. *Of course she is successful,* you want to scream. *She's so much more talented and driven and courageous and smart. She's got everything going for her, while I've got nothing.*

But have you ever stopped to think about what sets her and all of *those* people—those go-getters and accomplished few—apart from the rest of us? Have you ever wondered why they seem to have such an easy time reaching their dreams when it feels like you can't quite ever seem to pull yourself together?

I've been thinking about it a lot lately, and I *think* it has something to do with that long-term vision. The happiest, most successful, and most fulfilled people I know *do* have a secret road map for their lives. They've taken the time to visualize what their lives would look like if nothing stood in their way. They've given themselves enough freedom to dream about the future, and that dream gives them enough confidence to figure out a way to get there.

But the dream comes first.

Even if at the time you don't believe it is possible.

Way back when, in the midst of that devastating darkness of depression, I reluctantly wrote down that list of what I wanted my life to be like in ten years, I had absolutely *no reason* to believe—even for a second—that *any* of it could ever be possible. By that time I had lost everything. I was bankrupt and divorced, a college dropout with no job, no friends, and no future. I had been written off by nearly everyone I knew, and quite frankly, I couldn't blame them a bit. I was the poster child for hopeless causes.

But you know what? Fifteen or so years later—aside from *still* having the brownest thumb of anyone I've ever met (seriously, how can it be that hard to actually *grow* something?)—I've somehow managed to accomplish most of the items on that list *and then some*. What seemed downright impossible—things that seemed at the time too ridiculously absurd to even contemplate—eventually became somewhat plausible. Every now and then, I would take out that journal and reread the list, and as the years went by, the goals that were so far out of reach slowly evolved from plausible to possible, and then from possible to probable. Achieving those goals inspired me to create more goals and to make a whole *new* list of absurdly ridiculous dreams. So even when I lose my way sometimes—even in those moments when I get distracted or feel like I'm floundering—I've still got a road map that tells me where I'm going.

The Power of Writing It Down

Have you ever heard of a football coach named Lou Holtz? In 1966, when he was twenty-eight years old, Holtz was going through a serious rough patch. Not only was his coaching career going nowhere; he was broke and unemployed. To make matters worse, his wife was expecting their third child. Something had to give. Hoping to motivate him, his wife bought him a book called *The Magic of Thinking Big* by David Schwartz. The book worked. Inspired by what he read, Holtz decided that the key to changing his life was to *write down* the goals he really wanted to achieve. He realized that if he cared enough to write them down, he would somehow find a way to make them happen.

Holtz ended up writing down a list of 107 things in five different categories—things he wanted to achieve as a husband, things he wanted to do spiritually, things he wanted to achieve professionally, things he wanted to achieve financially, and things he wanted to do personally. Holtz's list included some pretty audacious goals, such as becoming the Notre Dame football coach, meeting the president of the United States, landing on an aircraft carrier, and appearing on *The Tonight Show*—crazy things that would have caused most people to laugh at him for even considering.

But guess what? Not only did Lou Holtz become the head football coach at Notre Dame, but he also led his team to a national championship. Among other things, he enjoyed dinner with Ronald Reagan at the White House, was a guest on *The Tonight Show*, met the pope, shot not one but *two* holes in one at golf, jumped out of an airplane, went on a safari in Africa, and, yes, he even landed on an aircraft carrier. To date, Lou Holtz has crossed off 102 of his 107 lifetime goals.[9]

While Lou Holtz turned out to be an awe-inspiring figure with an amazing, exceptional story to tell, he didn't start out that way. He was just an ordinary guy full of the same frustrations and failures and self-doubt we all experience at times. In fact, at one point his poor pregnant wife was wringing her hands just wondering how to get him off the couch! But ultimately the difference between Lou Holtz and so many others was that he became not only willing to *imagine* a better life for himself; he was also willing to *write it down*. Once he had written it down, he was able to take the necessary steps to make those goals happen.

It's not enough to have a vision *in your head* of what you wish your life could be. It's not enough to have some vague semblance or hazy daydream of what you'd like to accomplish *someday*. You have to actually take the time — whether it be five minutes or five hours — to *write it down*. Taking the time to write down your vision of the future not only forces you to self-evaluate and to decide what is most important, but it also motivates you to *act* on those dreams. Writing them down makes them real. And once they are real, you can't ignore them.

Planning Your Route

There's an old joke that asks the question, *How do you eat an elephant?* The answer, of course, is *one bite at a time.* The process of goal setting is a whole lot like figuring out how to eat that elephant, or, in this case, that long-term vision of what you want your life to look like down the road. Once you've got a clear destination in mind and you've clearly defined what your personal version of success looks like, the goals you set along the way will help determine exactly how you get there.

In addition to actually writing them down, which we've already talked about, here are a few practical tips I have found to be useful when it comes to effective and concrete goal setting:

- **Be clear about your objective.** This is where your vision comes into play. In other words, you have to know where you want to go before you can know how to get there. This idea is wonderfully illustrated in a scene from Lewis Carroll's classic, *Alice's Adventures in*

Wonderland, in which Alice stumbles upon the wise-but-cryptic Cheshire Cat, hoping for some direction:

"Would you tell me, please, which way I ought to go from here?"

"That depends a good deal on where you want to get to," said the Cat.

"I don't much care where—" said Alice.

"Then it doesn't matter which way you go," said the Cat.

"—so long as I get *somewhere*," Alice added as an explanation.

"Oh, you're sure to do that," said the Cat, "if you only walk long enough."[10]

Trying to move forward without first taking the time to clearly realize and write down your objectives probably won't accomplish much because you'll constantly be wondering where to go next. Whenever possible, your goals and objectives should be phrased in a way that is quantifiable so you can be crystal clear on whether or not you have achieved them. For instance, saying, *I want to lose weight* is not nearly as clear or quantifiable as saying, *I want to lose twenty pounds.*

- **Give yourself a due date.** Whether or not you mean it to, setting a specific completion date for your goals automatically creates a greater sense of urgency. Most of us are procrastinators by nature. We will often put off the hardest things until the last possible minute or until the repercussion of *not* doing something is worse than the pain of completing it. Just like setting a clear objective—*I want to lose twenty pounds*—helps clarify what we are aiming for, setting an arbitrary deadline—*I want to lose twenty pounds by March 31*—helps combat our tendency to procrastinate. It gives us just enough motivation to stop putting things off and start really getting things done. In fact, a goal without a deadline is just a pipe dream.

- **Break down large goals.** Big, lofty goals and crazily audacious dreams are wonderful, but if you truly want to reach them, you are going to have to tackle them in smaller bites. I am a firm believer in setting yearly goals, quarterly goals, monthly goals, weekly goals, and daily goals. Yearly goals are based on that pie-in-the-sky, long-term vision. They are the things I can do in the next twelve months that will get me closer to those big dreams of the future. Monthly goals, then, are based mostly on the goals set for the year. They are the things I can reasonably accomplish in the next thirty days that will get me closer to finishing everything on that yearly list. Likewise, weekly goals are based on those monthly goals, and the daily checklist reflects the things that need to be done each day in order to meet those goals for the week.

  For really big projects, such as writing a book, completing a project, or even planning a big party, I find it extremely helpful to put together a timeline of smaller goals. I start with the deadline, then work backward so I can have a series of small milestones leading up to the final completion date. This helps break it down in my mind so I am not overwhelmed by the largeness of the task. Each step on its own seems reasonable and doable. This process of breaking down big goals also helps me always know exactly what to be working on, and helps me avoid a false sense of security that I have plenty of time to get it done.

- **Track your progress.** The best way to stay focused on your goals is to continually monitor and measure your progress. Write down your goals in a place where you can refer to them often — every single day, if necessary. Goals that are scribbled in some random notebook that ends up at the bottom of your junk drawer won't be all that motivating. Create a poster for your office, put a chalkboard in your living room, write the goals in your planner, or post a list on your bathroom mirror so you can read them every time you brush your teeth. Do whatever it takes to put your list in a place that will force you to read and remember all the things you are working toward.

  Breaking down long-term goals into smaller steps and monthly, weekly, and daily goals also helps you stay on track because it constantly forces you to assess what you've done and what you still need to finish.

- **Create accountability.** Finding a person or a group of people to hold you accountable can make a huge difference, especially for those goals that require more self-discipline than you currently possess. If your goal is to run a marathon or a 5K race, join a local running group or a "Couch to 5K" group that will motivate you to actually get moving. If your goal is to straighten out your finances and get out of debt, try finding a local personal finance course (Dave Ramsey's Financial Peace University is a good one) to get support and instruction. I started my blog *Living Well Spending Less* because I thought public accountability would help me keep my out-of-control spending habits in check. Let me tell you — it worked!

Likewise, for the past few years I have found that having an accountability partner really helps keep me on track. My accountability partner Edie and I talk almost every day and are completely honest with one another about our struggles, weaknesses, and aspirations. As a fellow blogger at LifeinGraceBlog .com, she understands firsthand the unique demands of our profession. She challenges me, encourages me, and prays for me, and I do the same for her. If there is someone in your life you trust or admire, consider asking them to be an accountability partner.

- **Celebrate your success.** There is nothing quite as satisfying as checking a big task off your list — especially one you weren't sure you'd be able to accomplish. Take the time to savor those moments, to revel in the triumph of actually *doing* it. Be sure to make time to celebrate not just the big accomplishments and major milestones but the small victories too. Don't be afraid to congratulate yourself for a job well done.

Goal Setting for a Better Marriage

Over the years I have also come to realize that setting specific goals as a *couple* is an important part of a healthy and happy marriage. I don't know how it works in your marriage, but I have discovered that my husband and I are never so solid as when we are working together toward a common goal, whether it be renovating a house, repairing our hurricane damage, or getting out of debt.

They say opposites attract, and for the most part, my husband and I are as different as night and day. Our tastes in food, clothing, television shows, and, well, pretty much everything else couldn't be farther apart. In fact, not long ago we even took a couples' personality test that totally confirmed our suspicions. Out of the four possible personality types, Chuck was evenly split across the board. He is as steady as they come, patient and methodical and thorough to a fault. An engineer through and through, he sees the world in terms of problems that need rational solutions. He's not easily excitable, and he always weighs the pros and cons of every option. Sometimes endlessly.

And then there's me. Unlike Chuck, my skill set peaked in one particular personality column. I am the leader, the go-getter, the driven one. I make snap decisions—or impulsive ones, depending on your point of view—and am perfectly happy telling everyone else exactly what needs to be done. I am goal-oriented and self-motivated, but also impatient, overly blunt, and somewhat irrational.

Not surprisingly, given my tendency to always be striving for just a little bit more and Chuck's tendency to, well, *not,* we have often found ourselves at odds. I think he's too laid-back, not trying hard enough, while he wishes I would just *relax* every now and then. I have to admit that I have been guilty on more than one occasion of setting goals for myself and for my own career that weren't exactly in line with what my husband envisioned for our family, often to disastrous results. The more I strived toward my own goals, the more frustrated and angry he became.

After more than a few heated discussions—and perhaps even one or two knock-down, drag-out fights—I began to slowly and reluctantly accept the fact that as a mom and a wife, my goals can't be simply *my* goals. For better or for worse, they are *our* goals. I finally realized that if I am committed to making our family work and thrive, then I must also be committed to finding common ground with my husband and creating a shared vision for our life together.

Eventually we made a priority to spend some time writing down together the things we want to do within the next five years. Most of it was practical stuff, but we even threw in a few crazy, audacious dreams to strive for together. Then we broke our list down into the things we needed to accomplish in the next year, and we wrote that list on a big chalkboard in our kitchen so we can both look at it every single day.

Friends, let me tell you, it is pretty amazing to discover how much the dynamics of your relationship can change when you are suddenly striving together toward the same goal. The day-to-day conflicts—especially for couples like us, who are as different as night and day—are so much easier to handle when you realize you are in this together, and you are in it for the long haul.

Short-Term Sacrifices
for Long-Term Gain

This reality of shared goals has certainly been true when it comes to our family vehicle. Although we have owned newer and flashier cars over the years, my husband and I currently share a 2002 Chevy Tahoe that just hit the 150,000 mile mark. While I certainly wouldn't call it a *junker*—at least not yet—it is also not quite up to par with the shiny new Honda Odysseys, Nissan Pathfinders, and Lincoln Navigators next to us in the parent pickup line. The leather seats are cracked, and each year adds a few dents and scratches to the once-pristine exterior, blemishes we now try to view as character. While I have no doubt there are more than a few parents in that line who turn up their noses at our humble ride, *they don't see what we see.* We see a car that since 2004 has taken us cross-country no less than five different times, a car that has been off-road in Arches National Park, climbed Mount Rainier, trekked through Death Valley, nearly been driven off a cliff, and has even seen us through a hurricane. We see a car that is totally reliable, never giving us a moment's grief in all those years, and even more importantly, *we see a vehicle that has never had a car payment.*

Having a long-term vision and written goals hasn't just changed our personal and professional lives, but has made all the difference when it comes to our financial life too. An important shift happened when we began making money decisions based on what we wanted to accomplish five, ten, or twenty years from now rather than on what we wanted or what we think would make us happy right now. Dave

Ramsey calls it "living like no one else, so later you can live like no one else," and he is exactly right. Setting long-term goals empowers us to delay gratification so we can achieve them. My husband and I are willing to endure a few disdainful glances, however subtle, because we know this short-term sacrifice will help us reach our long-term goals. It has been more important to pay off debt, establish an emergency fund, pay for college, and plan for retirement than it is to meet the approval of those parents who may barely be scraping together their car payments each month. We *love* our beat-up Tahoe, not just because of where it has been, but because of where it is taking us.

Where to Start

Even if I've managed to convince you how important and life-changing it can be to set concrete, written goals, you may still be feeling a little overwhelmed by the idea, particularly if you've never tried it before. Where should you even start? What goals should you choose? How do you narrow your focus? How many goals should you make? What is the best way to prioritize? How do you make time for the goals you've selected?

If you are struggling to know where to begin, I think it helps to follow Lou Holtz's lead and break down your goals and vision into different categories. What sort of wife and mother do you want to be? What kind of marriage and family life do you want to have? What milestones would you like to reach in your faith walk and in your church? What impact would you like to have on your community or on the world? What would you like to accomplish in your career and professional life? What awards, promotions, or degrees would you like to receive? What sort of financial goals do you have? Would you like to pay off your house, get rid of debt, or establish an emergency fund? Do you want to save for retirement or set up college funds for your children? What fun things do you want to do with your life? Where would you like to go? What would you like to see? Who would you like to meet? What would you like to read?

Start by writing down anything and everything you can think of, from those crazy, audacious, impossible-sounding dreams to the little things you could probably do tomorrow if you really wanted to. Give yourself the freedom to dream big and to get it all out on paper. From there you can begin to break down that big list into "someday," "within ten years," "within five years," and "within the next year" categories, and then break down those one-year goals even further into goals for the next month, week, and day.

On my blog I offer a printable eleven-page goal-setting workbook that can walk you through the process of determining your priorities, setting specific goals, combating procrastination, developing good habits, and eliminating the things that don't matter. It is a great resource, whether you are a seasoned goal setter who just wants to get refocused, or whether you have never before considered creating a long-term vision for your life. You can get it at www.living wellspendingless.com/goalworkbook or by scanning the QR code on this page.

No matter who we are or where

we're going, there will always be distractions along the way. It may be a change in routine, an unexpected obstacle, or, as in my case, suddenly having a husband at home full-time. While I did struggle mightily for a month or two, I found that as soon as I took the time to get refocused on my long-term vision and to write down some new concrete goals for the future, everything began to once again fall into place. I suddenly had direction and clarity for what needed to be done. I was reminded, once again, that written goals truly are an antidote to life's setbacks. They are the secret road map that can keep you on track and prevent anything from standing in your way. Written goals can change your life.

CHALLENGE: **Plan Your Long-Term Vision**

Grab a cup of coffee and a notebook and give yourself some time to think and pray about your long-term goals and dreams. What would you like your life to look like ten years from now? What sort of things would you like to achieve in your personal, professional, and spiritual life? Don't just think about these goals; *write them down!*

Next, make a date with your spouse to spend some time discussing your long-term vision for your life together. Give yourselves permission to dream big and to be honest about what you'd like to do or see or accomplish in the future. Create a plan and then *write down* your goals in a place where you can both see them.

Finally, break down that long-term vision you've created into shorter-term goals. What are five things you want to accomplish in the next year? What are five things you want to accomplish in the next month? Use my printable goal-setting workbook if you feel overwhelmed.

We All Get the Same Twenty-Four Hours

Things that matter most should never be at the mercy of things that matter least.

Johann Wolfgang von Goethe

For the Spirit God gave us does not make us timid, but gives us power, love and self-discipline.

2 Timothy 1:7

Time is what we want most but what we use worst.

William Penn

I will be the first to admit I am often my own worst enemy when it comes to buckling down and doing all those things I know I should do. In fact, the mere *thought* of writing a chapter on time management and self-discipline makes me cringe when I think of all the areas in my life in which I still lack so much willpower.

For instance, as much I love the *idea* of maintaining a fresh, healthy, and all-organic whole food diet, and as fond as I am of the thought of filling my body with nothing but fruits, veggies, and unprocessed "real" foods, the reality is that I am secretly a junk food junkie. I confiscate my kids' Easter and Halloween candy in order to fill up my own secret chocolate stash. I sometimes eat nothing but ice cream for dinner. I am a vegetarian who hates salad, and I recently asked my husband if he thought it would be okay to eat pizza every night. I was completely serious.

The craziest part of it all is that I genuinely *enjoy* cooking great food on those rare occasions I can actually manage to muster up the energy for it. I'm even a pretty darn good cook, if I do say so myself, creative and confident and good at coming up with new recipes that taste terrific. I don't *dislike* healthy food; on the contrary, I can honestly say I prefer it. If someone else were making it for me, I would almost always choose a healthy, home-cooked meal over pizza, and I'd *probably* even choose it over ice cream.

The problem, of course, is that someone else *isn't* making it for me. While it remains a life goal, I have yet to find a personal chef willing to work for free. By the time dinnertime rolls around, I have already been going strong for twelve solid hours. I've already spent the whole day working, running errands, shuttling kids to dance class or soccer, and fitting in chores wherever I can. Most of the time I feel like I've got nothing left. And so we eat pizza. Or cereal. Or ice cream. Again.

And then, of course, I step on the scale and immediately regret all those poor choices. *Oh, if only I had more willpower!*

I think sometimes our tendency is to view self-discipline as a genetically predetermined quality or character trait. Deep down, we believe some of us are born with it and some of us aren't. We see all those supermoms around us who seem to have it all together, and we assume they were the ones born with the time management gene. And then, when we fail to eat the healthy foods we know we should, can't manage to get up early and exercise, or spend the whole day surfing the web when we intended to actually get something done, our suspicions are confirmed. We say to ourselves, *I guess I don't have it. It's just the way I am.*

But what if it's not?

What if self-discipline and time management skills are something that can be strengthened over time? What if self-control is not an innate character trait bestowed on a select few, but something we all need to develop? What if willpower is actually a finite quality, one that runs out over the course of the day? Wouldn't that change the game? Wouldn't we want to be sure we used our energies well?

Eating Our Frogs

I read a book a few years ago that forever changed the way I approached my daily task list. It's called *Eat That Frog!: 21 Great Ways to Stop Procrastinating and Get More Done in Less Time*.[11] The book gets its name from a quote often attributed to Mark Twain: "If the first thing you do each morning is to eat a live frog, you can be pretty sure it's the worst thing that will happen to you all day long. And if it's your job to eat two frogs, it's best to eat the biggest one first." The point of the quote—and the book—was that if you start your day by tackling your hardest but most important tasks, you will have already done a lot—even if you don't do much of anything else for the whole rest of the day.

Life moves fast, and it is so very easy to get sucked into the mundane—albeit essential—tasks of the everyday. We often spend the bulk of our day putting out fires, responding to needs, or escaping into the time-wasting vortex of social media and email. It all seems so important, so urgent, but before we know it, we've spent the whole day reacting to other people rather than proactively working to accomplish the things we really want to do.

The main problem with living our lives this way is that our willpower runs out. Each morning we start our day filled with a certain amount of self-discipline, and as we go about our day, that resolve tends to drain out. When we start our day by focusing on the mundane and easy stuff, we waste our reserves. Eating our frogs first thing in the morning means having enough energy and discipline to truly get the important things done.

As we discovered in the last chapter, written goals are usually what separates the go-getters and accomplished few from those who are for the most part just getting by. While having a solid vision and a written plan for what we'd like to achieve is essential, it is also important to remember that *goals are just the beginning.* Achieving those goals requires action. Our life is only as good as our goals, but self-discipline is the key to achieving them.

Lou Holtz, after writing down his list of overly ambitious life aspirations, didn't just sit around waiting for something to happen. He began working as hard as he could every single day in order to realize his dreams. With three young kids at home and an uncertain future, he could easily have been caught up in the day-to-day drudgery of just getting by. Facing poverty, he might have accepted any job he could get that would keep food on the table. It would have been easy to settle for ordinary. No one would have blamed him for simply trying to provide for his family.

But he didn't stop at just getting food on the table. With his list in hand as a constant, physical reminder of the bigger picture, he put his head down and began doing everything he could to accomplish his goals. He worked diligently, not just on the tasks that would pay the bills, but on the ones that would get him closer to his dreams. Every single day he made a conscious decision to put his most important tasks first — to do those things first that would make the biggest difference later on. Lou Holtz became very good at eating frogs.

On any given day, we all have our own frogs to tackle. If we are serious about attaining our goals and following through on our dreams—no matter what those dreams may be—then we must also make the daily choice to do something, anything, to get us one small step closer to the finish line. We have to be purposeful about making sure the big stuff gets done first. We must accept the truth that if we don't take the time to put our long-term goals first, *there will never be enough time or energy for our dreams.* The obligations of the everyday will always take over. How would your life be different one year from now if you were willing to take the first thirty minutes of your day to work only on long-term goals?

Creating Good Habits

Our brains are wired to form habits. In his book *The Power of Habit*, Charles Duhigg explains that these habits can be good or bad, but once something has become a true habit, a different part of our brain takes over and we begin to perform that particular task on autopilot.[12] This means we no longer have to use mental energy to think about forcing ourselves to do the task or to actually perform the task itself, which leaves our brain free to focus on getting more important things done, and frees up our willpower to be used on our more difficult tasks.

After reading *The Power of Habit*, I realized that creating good habits was the key to being able to get things done. The more good habits I could create for myself, the more willpower and mental energy I would have left over to pursue my dreams. If I could make doing all the things I needed to do in the morning a *habit*, something that happened automatically without even thinking, the autopilot portion of my brain would kick in and I would have more discipline stored up to tackle the rest of my to-do list. Instead of feeling frustrated because my morning would start well but then I'd just sort of fizzle out in the afternoon, I could create routines that allowed me to stay focused all day long. And by the time evening rolled around, I would still have energy left to actually cook a healthy dinner for my family! It sounded almost too good to be true, but I was ready to try.

I made a list of all the habits I wanted to do automatically every morning. My list started with drinking a tall glass of water as soon as I woke up, then taking ten minutes to plan my day over a cup of coffee. This was followed by personal-devotion-and-prayer time, then writing for at least ninety minutes. Amazingly enough, after several weeks of doing this every single day, I stopped thinking about it. I would find myself in the kitchen drinking my water before I was even fully awake, and I discovered it was taking almost no mental effort to get my day started off right. By the end of my ninety-minute writing session, when I was ready to take a morning break, I would still feel refreshed and ready to conquer my day.

For months after developing this simple routine, I was more productive than I had ever been before. I had never felt more confident or capable. I was sure I had figured out the secret to getting more done in less time. I was using my twenty-four hours well.

And then we went on vacation. Not just any vacation, but a monthlong, four-thousand-mile family road trip. We spent twenty-nine days touring the country—seeing some incredible sites and visiting with friends and family all along the way. It was the trip of a lifetime, one my husband and I had dreamed about taking for years. We created countless memories that I will cherish forever.

But that trip killed my groove.

We arrived home and jumped head first into a whole new schedule, one that included a new school and a new job and a whole new list of responsibilities and obligations. My carefully crafted morning plan fell apart, and before I really knew what had happened, I fell apart too. I completely lost my mojo. Suddenly I was once again having trouble staying focused and managing my time well. In fact, most days I felt like I had fizzled out before I even began.

I struggled for months to establish a new routine. I once again found myself reacting to the circumstances of any given day rather than proactively setting up a new pattern of daily habits to follow. Every day became a grind, and no matter how well I started, by the end of the day I was exhausted. Frustrated and fed up with my lack of discipline, I knew it was time to reevaluate my schedule. I needed to figure out what *wasn't* working for me so I could create a new routine that *would* work. I just wasn't sure what to do.

Finally one evening I decided to swallow my pride and ask my husband for advice. It was a big step, because until that moment, I had been trying to figure it out all on my own. I admitted to him — and myself — that I was really struggling. We talked for a while, and together we determined that one of my biggest problems was that I had stopped getting up early and was staying up too late. I was literally sleeping through the part of the day when my brain works best. We agreed to make some major changes that would help get me back on track.

I once again made a list of the habits I wanted to establish in my morning routine, starting with the time I'd get out of bed. I wrote down *every single step*, including getting dressed, making a cup of coffee, having devotions and prayer time, and all the other details of my morning work routine. I was as detailed as possible, even though it felt a little silly to write down things like "use the bathroom." Did I *really* need to remind myself to do that? But I wrote it all down, not because I didn't know how to do it, but because I wanted to do it *the exact same way every morning*. With a written list, I could just follow the steps in order until they became a habit. The minute my alarm went off, I would be ready to go.

But I didn't stop there. I also concluded that for me as a morning person, it was even more essential to establish a strong evening routine. I tend to fade into uselessness after six o'clock at night, but I knew I could be doing some important things in the evening to help ensure a better morning, such as taking fifteen minutes to pick up the house, setting out my clothes, making a to-do list for the following day, and even showering. Knowing just how unmotivated I am in the evening, I also enlisted the help of my husband to encourage me and to keep me on track, and I told him that, *no matter what*, he had to make sure I was in bed by ten o'clock.

I'm not going to lie. It was a rough couple of weeks. Establishing a new routine was even harder the second time around, and there were times when it felt downright painful. Many mornings I really, *really* wanted to sleep in, and more than a few evenings I wanted nothing more than to stay up until midnight watching Netflix. Through it all, my husband was my rock, the one who held me accountable and encouraged me to keep going when I wanted to give up.

And then eventually, a few weeks into the new schedule, it wasn't *quite* so hard anymore. Getting up early wasn't quite so painful; after a while it even began to feel *normal*. The new habits began to take hold, and I found I no longer needed to refer to my lists. I could complete all the steps automatically, without even thinking about them. Even more amazingly, I once again had time and energy to spare. I had more quality time to spend with my kids and husband, and even found that cooking dinner wasn't quite such a chore. (At least some of the time!)

While it seems almost too good to be true, the fact is that the more we shift into autopilot, the more willpower reserve we will have left for the things that matter. If you are anything like me, the idea of good time management is a daunting task, one that seems overwhelming and practically impossible. The pressure of using those precious twenty-four hours well can be too much to bear. On the other hand, establishing just a few crucial habits is something anyone can do without all that much effort. Our habits will ultimately determine what we get done. Make them count.

Eliminating the Unessential

Getting rid of the things I don't really need to be doing is the hardest part of managing my time. I am very good at overcommitting, and even better at spending countless hours doing things that don't really need to be done. I'm fairly certain I'm not alone. Every single one of us probably has a few time fillers or time wasters we could stand to eliminate from our day. It might be something as simple as baking cookies from scratch when Oreos would've sufficed, or spending an hour (or four) watching television or drooling over Pinterest. It could even be something nobler, such as leading a committee you don't really have time for, or agreeing to attend a birthday party when you already have three other things scheduled for that day.

Eliminating the unessential is where setting priorities and having a long-term vision become so vitally important. If, when we look at our day, we find that too much of our time is filled with things that don't align with our priorities or most important goals, then something has to give. As important as it is to establish good habits and patterns for the things we do want to do, it is equally important to eliminate those things that are taking up time but not adding value.

What would happen if you spent the next week writing down every single thing you did? Would you find that your time log matched the priorities you established in chapter 2, or the goals you wrote down in chapter 4? What would happen if someone else were to observe how you use your time? Would your long-term vision be immediately apparent? Does the way you use your time clearly reflect what is most important to you?

It is *hard* to say no sometimes, especially when it means disappointing someone or denying ourselves the opportunity to do something we enjoy. In today's society, the temptation to pile on more and more until we are completely overwhelmed is always present. There are more committees, more sports, more hobbies, more obligations, more distractions, more channels, more charities, and more of, well, pretty much everything than ever before. And the maddening thing is that it all sounds so good!

- *Of course we'll participate in this year's Christmas pageant. Practices are twice a week for the next three months? Well, we'll find some way to work it out.*

- *The school needs ten dozen cupcakes? By tomorrow? No problem!*

- *Birthday party at three o'clock on Saturday? We'll be there! Oh, wait—we might be a little late. We've got soccer. Then violin lessons. And then Girl Scouts. And one other birthday party. But we look forward to it!*

There will always be more activities than we have time for, and far more opportunities and temptations and obligations than we can ever reasonably hope to manage. If we were to be totally honest with ourselves, I'm pretty sure most of us could name at least a few activities that currently take up a significant amount of time in our lives but don't add a whole lot of value. We all have to make choices in life about what we will and will not do with our time. In fact, we are *already* making choices every single day. The question is, *Do our choices match our calling—our vision, goals, passion, and dreams?*

Giving Ourselves Grace

A few years ago, I woke up on a Monday morning ready to start my week with a bang. I had spent the weekend getting caught up and prepared for the week ahead, and by 8:00 a.m., with several hours of work under my belt, I was feeling pretty good about my day. I still had a whole list of things left to accomplish, but I was off to a great start. I just knew it was going to be an awesomely productive day.

And then I got a text message from a Very Important Person asking if I would be available for a phone call.

I don't know how it works in your family, but my children have an amazing sixth sense that tells them they suddenly need everything in the world right at the exact moment the phone rings. Since I knew I wouldn't want to be disturbed during this Very Important Phone Call, I did the essential Very Important Phone Call prep: I prepared snacks and water, made sure both girls had gone potty, and then gave my oldest daughter, who was five at the time, a long pep talk about how, as the older child, she needed to be an example and Mommy's big helper and under *no circumstances* was she to come out of her room or let her sister bother Mommy while Mommy was on the Very Important Phone Call.

And then I waited. The hour came and went with no call. And then another hour came and went. While the phone eventually did ring and the Very Important Phone Call was successfully completed with not a single interruption, by the time it was finally over, the entire morning was shot and all my perfect plans for a productive morning had gone awry.

The reason I remember that day so clearly is that I

realized in that moment—perhaps for the first time—I had a choice. I could have easily spent the rest of the day running around like a mad woman, frantically trying to get every last item checked off my list, most likely yelling at my poor kids to cooperate in the process, and completely over-looking the fact that by some miracle they had just spent the last two and a half hours playing quietly in their room. But thankfully that's not what I did. Instead of getting stressed, I adjusted my expectations for the day. I reevaluated the things that *had* to be done versus the things that *could* be done, crossed several items off my list, and then spent the next few hours giggling with my daughters as we worked together to deep-clean their room. Then we ran some errands, and I even found a few minutes to stop for cupcakes. No, I didn't get it all done, but it was a very good day just the same.

Every once in a while, someone will ask me how I am able to do it all. "How do you manage it?" they'll ask. "What's your secret? You must be Superwoman."

If only they knew! I'm pretty sure Superwoman at least managed to take a shower once in a while! The fact is that, although I have moments here and there where I feel pretty super, more often than not the nitty-gritty details of life bring me back down to reality with an earth-shattering crash. Even so, as I get a little older—and hopefully a little wiser—I am learning to roll with the punches a bit more. Having a few ground rules in place for taking back my time has helped a lot too:

- **Know your priorities.** We've already talked a lot about priorities, but when there is too much to do, knowing what things are truly important helps dictate your daily to-do list (and deviations from it). Keep a list of what matters most and refer to it daily.

- **Start your morning well.** Create a consistent morning routine that kick-starts your day on the right track. For me, starting the day with a few minutes of prayer and reflection over a cup of fresh, hot coffee makes all the difference in the world. Other morning rituals include planning my day, making the bed, and tackling my hardest task first.

- **Prep for success.** Taking just a few minutes in the evening to prepare for the next day—by picking out the next day's clothes, making lunches, doing a little tidying up, or making sure the dishes are done—can be the difference between a smooth start and all-out chaos. Likewise, spending a few hours on Sunday evening doing laundry, cooking, or cleaning can create a momentum that lasts all week.

- **Give yourself grace.** On the days when my schedule goes exactly as planned and I get everything checked off my list, I feel pretty good about myself. But those days are very rare. In fact, they are almost nonexistent. The rest of the time I am constantly having to readjust my expectations, reprioritize my task list, and give myself a whole lot of grace.

- **Give your time to God.** One of the reasons I start my morning in prayer and devotion is that it helps bring clarity and focus to my day. I will often find that the perfect Scripture verse just seems to pop out at me or the devotional I'm reading seems to tie in perfectly to a dilemma I've been wrestling with. Ultimately there is something very freeing about starting my day with the words, *Lord, let this all be for you.*

I was once chatting with a friend and bemoaning the fact that a mutual friend of ours seemed to have it all, while I was more or less a mess. There she was — with her perfect job and perfect kids, always on top of things and always totally put together, while I'm the mom who is always running late, whose kids run around naked half the time and do crazy things like walk headfirst into the counter or color all over themselves with markers. I'm the mom who neglects to return phone calls and who misses show-and-tell day and snack day, the one whose dog runs away because I forget I let her out, and who misses important events because I can't always keep it all straight.

My sweet friend, who is far wiser than me, responded with something so profound that it has been stuck in my head ever since. She said, "Don't you know that everyone gets the same twenty-four hours?" She went on to explain that while from the outside looking in, all might seem perfect, there is no such thing as Superwoman. No one can do everything all the time without letting something else slide. And it doesn't make us any less wonderful; it just makes us *human.*

Self-discipline and time management skills are wonderful tools — ones we can and should work to develop and strengthen. It is ultimately our willingness to *do* the hard things on our list and to create good habits and daily routines that will get us to our goals. Even so, we have to be willing to give ourselves the grace to know we can't always do it all. Keep in sight what matters most, and the rest will fall into place.

CHALLENGE: Take Back Your Time

For one week, make a commitment to get up thirty minutes earlier than normal and spend that time working on one of the major goals you established in chapter 4. At the end of the week, evaluate your progress. What were you able to accomplish in that time? Was it more or less than you thought you could do? Did this process inspire you to make any other changes in your life?

Make a list of three things you want to do first thing in the morning, and three things you want to do before bedtime. Copy this list and put it on your nightstand, bathroom mirror, refrigerator, or any other place you will see it often. Do the things on your list every day until they become automatic, and then add additional steps to your routine as necessary.

Finally, take an honest look at your current schedule. Does the way you spend your time truly reflect your priorities? Is there anything you could eliminate from your day completely? What adjustments could you make to your morning, evening, and weekend routines that would help your days flow more smoothly?

Less Stuff Equals More Joy

Have nothing in your houses that you don't know to be useful, or believe to be beautiful.

William Morris

I have learned to be content whatever the circumstances. I know what it is to be in need, and I know what it is to have plenty. I have learned the secret of being content in any and every situation, whether well fed or hungry, whether living in plenty or in want. I can do all this through him who gives me strength.

Philippians 4:11–13

"Sell your possessions and give to the poor. Provide purses for yourselves that will not wear out, a treasure in heaven that will never fail, where no thief comes near and no moth destroys. For where your treasure is, there your heart will be also."

Luke 12:33–34

There was stuff *everywhere*.

As much as I would've liked to point the finger elsewhere, there was no one but myself to blame for the chaotic mess that our life had become. Yes, my girls were being showered with gifts from a very generous auntie who showed her love by providing more toys and books and art supplies and dresses than they could ever possibly use, but I was just as guilty—if not *more*—of filling our house to the brim with the really *nice* stuff that we *really* didn't need. A simple trip to Target would inevitably result in a cute new dish towel or a picture frame or a limited edition pair of rain boots from the latest designer-inspired line. I could barely open a Pottery Barn catalog without needing just one more lamp, one more rug, one more pillow.

The combination of my own shopping addiction and my sister-in-law's generosity was practically lethal. And then, finally, I woke up one morning and realized we were literally *drowning* in stuff.

Something had to give.

I started a mission to purge the chaos in our life and start getting rid of all the excess stuff we had accumulated, but it was slow going. Our home was not filled with junk; it was filled to the brim with *really* nice stuff that we *really* didn't need. It is easy to purge things that are broken or damaged or old or junky, but it is a lot harder to justify eliminating things that are still useful or valuable. It seems so wasteful. Over the course of several months, I slowly began weeding out my girls' toys, trying to keep only the items they actually played with and that encouraged their imaginations.

Even so, there were warning signs that my kids still had too much stuff. One weekend we took the girls to Reptile World in Orlando. Afterward we thought it would be fun to have dinner in the dinosaur-themed restaurant, T-Rex, in Downtown Disney. While we were waiting for a table, six-year-old Maggie spotted the Build-A-Dino workshop in the gift shop and begged to go in. We immediately said no way, but from that moment on, she could think of nothing else. Throughout our delicious dinner, surrounded by dramatic meteor showers and animatronic dinosaur shows, she fixated on the one thing she couldn't have rather than on the incredible sights she was experiencing. She was too busy pouting to enjoy herself.

On the three-hour drive home, worried by Maggie's inability to enjoy what should have been a fun experience, we made a point to talk about all the neat stuff we had seen that day. We talked about our favorite reptiles and how funny it was that Annie had wanted to hold the boa constrictor three times—and even given the snake a *kiss*! By the time we made it home, Build-A-Dino had been forgotten. At least by her. But we were worried.

In the weeks that followed, Chuck and I talked a lot about how to handle this lack of contentment we were noticing in our eldest daughter. Then one morning, a few weeks after our Orlando trip and about six months after I had started my mission to simplify our lives, I made the semi-impulsive decision to take away *all* the kids' toys. I had warned them repeatedly that if they couldn't keep their room tidy, the toys would go away. I wasn't asking them to clean a giant, out-of-control mess—I had just reorganized their room two days earlier—but simply to pick up a few items from the floor and put them away in the very clearly labeled baskets.

After asking them to pick up for the umpteenth time, I finally decided enough was enough. I gave up and took it all away. I wasn't really angry—just fed up—and I calmly began packing up not just a toy or two but every single thing. All their dress-up clothes, baby dolls, Polly Pockets, and stuffed animals. All their Barbies, building blocks, toy trains, and Littlest Pet Shop animals, right down to the furniture in their dollhouse and the play food in their kitchen. I even took the pretty Pottery Barn comforter off their bed, leaving them with just the plain white sheets and blanket underneath. The girls watched in stunned silence for a few minutes, and then, after the shock wore off, they helped pack it all up.

Just like that, the room was clear.

Paradigm Shift

I could never have predicted what a dramatic difference this one decision would make in all of our lives, but we first started noticing a real change about four weeks later when we took the girls on a family trip to Key West. In contrast to our previous outing, and perhaps for the first time ever, neither daughter asked us to buy a single thing the entire weekend. Not a toy, not a cheesy souvenir, not a light-up necklace from a passing street vendor. Nothing. We passed hundreds of shops, and they loved looking in the windows—but they were content just to *be*. What was most amazing to me was that we hadn't instructed them not to ask for anything. They did it all on their own.

Had I not experienced it with my own eyes, I would have never believed that an addiction to stuff could be broken so fast. When I took all their toys away, I was terrified at what might happen. I worried that I was possibly scarring them for life, depriving them of some essential developmental need, or taking away their ability to self-entertain.

In reality, the opposite happened. Instead of being bored, they suddenly had no shortage of things to do. Their attention span grew longer, and they were more able to mindfully focus on the task at hand. They were able to read or color for hours at a time (they still had access to books and art supplies) and would happily spend the entire afternoon playing hide-and-seek or making up an elaborate and imaginative game. They became far more content, more able to appreciate the things they did have, and more able to enjoy the moment without feeling the constant need to move on to the next thing. They became more patient, more willing to share, and far more empathetic toward the plight of others. They even, for the most part, stopped fighting with each other. Their friends seemed to enjoy coming over more, and more than once we overheard playmates asking their parents if they, too, could get rid of some toys.

Even more importantly, they seemed better able to recognize excess on their own. Even when they were given the ability to earn some of their toys back, they didn't really want them, at least not on a permanent basis. They wanted their American Girl dolls and a few special stuffed animals, and we kept Legos and a few Barbies on the shelf to play with on occasion. Overall, however, they genuinely *liked* not being overwhelmed by so much stuff, and they were happy to not have to spend so much time cleaning up. In fact, a few hours later on that day I took their toys away, my oldest daughter said, "It's okay that we don't have any more toys, Mommy. We can just read and use our imaginations. And now we won't have to clean up so much!" She understood before I did that more stuff doesn't make us happier.

When I first became a mom, I was so happy to have a chance to start over and to undo through my children all the mistakes and regrets of my past. I was eager to give them everything I felt I had missed out on. I wanted our lives to be perfect, and my vision of perfection included a perfectly decorated bedroom filled with beautiful things and a life where they would want for nothing. I equated giving them stuff with making them happy, a message our consumer-driven culture hammers into our psyches from the time we are born.

Oh, what a lie!

There are so many times when I buy things because I am bored or unhappy, just to fill the void. I often talk a good game about wanting to downsize and simplify and purge my life of excess, but there are still, even now, many times when I just can't stop myself from buying more. I justify it, telling myself it was on sale or a really good deal or something we really needed, or that I deserve it because I work so hard. In reality it is just another thing I am buying to try to solve a problem that runs so much deeper.

Stuff isn't bad or dangerous in and of itself, but in a world where we are constantly told that what we have isn't quite good enough, the love of things can so easily consume us. The pursuit of it all—more toys, cuter clothes, a prettier house, a nicer car, a newer computer, a fancier phone—makes us forget all the things that actually matter.

Not until I observed firsthand the real and immediate changes in my kids after getting rid of their toys did I truly begin to understand. My lesson to them was really their lesson to me, one I wish I would have learned a long time ago. Less stuff equals more joy.

Clearing the Clutter

Of course, wanting to have less and actually accomplishing this feat are two totally different things. Chuck and I found out the hard way that the process of accumulating a house full of stuff is much easier than the process of letting it go. Don't get me wrong, on a day-to-day basis, our comfortable, little, three-bedroom, two-bathroom house appears relatively neat and clean and clutter free. Organized even. The dishes are washed, and the clutter is picked up and put, well, somewhere. But all that STUFF is lurking in the background, tucked away behind closed doors, in closets and cupboards and containers. And in the garage. Especially in the garage.

Our progress is at times painfully slow. For most of our marriage Chuck and I have been at odds when it comes to the acquisition and loss of property. My philosophy has always been "easy come, easy go." The shopaholic in me loves to bring it in, but the neat freak in me loves to see it go. Chuck, on the other hand, hates to shop and buys almost nothing. He will literally do almost anything to avoid having to set foot in a store. But once it was in our house — courtesy of yours truly — he couldn't stand to see it tossed out. To him, it was wastefulness. He wasn't wrong.

The problem was that the combination of our differing personalities basically turned our home into a black hole. Once something came in, it could never, ever leave. Ultimately our catalyst for real and lasting change was taking away the girls' toys. Seeing the dramatic change in them — the contentment and joy that came from purging so much excess — forever changed the way I looked at stuff. After so many years of trying to fill a void with material possessions, I was finally, *finally* able to stop shopping. And when I finally stopped bringing more in, Chuck was finally able to let things go.

For the first time ever, we were able to work together to start clearing all the clutter we — mostly I — had accumulated. It felt so good! The more we got rid of, the more we wanted to get rid of. We found that decluttering begets more decluttering. It was overwhelming at first, and with so much stuff to go through, the process has taken a really long time. I'm not sure we'll ever fully be done.

Even so, we've discovered quite a few helpful tricks for becoming and *staying* clutter free. If your home is in need of purging, you may want to try these strategies:

- **Do an initial sweep.** Grab a box and a large garbage bag, and starting at one side, do a walk-through of your entire house. Scan each room for clutter, quickly grabbing anything you see that you know is either garbage or no longer needed. Only grab the things that are out in the open — don't worry yet about sifting through drawers or closets — and either throw away the items you find or add them to the donation box. Keep going until you've made it through the entire house. This is a fairly easy and painless process that will allow you to make a lot of progress in a very short time.

- **Focus on one area at a time.** Once you've completed an initial surface purge, it is time to dig a little deeper. Please trust me when I say it is not a good idea to start randomly delving into more than one area at a time. You will quickly become overwhelmed! Instead, start with one small and manageable area — a single room or corner, a closet, a cabinet, or a dresser — armed with a box to collect donation items, a laundry basket to collect things that should be returned to their proper place, and a garbage bag for the trash. Then get to work and don't leave your area until the job is done.

- **Ruthlessly purge.** Give yourself permission to keep only the things that are currently useful — never mind who gave them to you or how much they cost. This can be really hard, especially at first. This is where the ruthless part comes in. As you sort through your things, ask yourself these questions:
  - Do we use it, wear it, or play with it?
  - Or, if it is clothing, does it still fit?
  - Is it in good working condition?

— Does it enrich our lives in some way?
— Does it have sentimental value?
— Could someone else use it more?

I think it is helpful to create four categories or piles for the items you are sorting. The first pile should be the items that need to stay in the same general area but may simply need to be rearranged or organized once all the clutter is gone. The second pile should be donation items and can go directly into your donation box. The third category is trash, which should go directly into the garbage bag. The fourth and final category is things that need to be put elsewhere. Use a large laundry basket to collect these items and put them away before moving on to another area of the house. Then repeat, repeat, repeat!

- **Get it out of your house.** Once you've determined something needs to go, get rid of it as quickly as possible. Don't let the boxes of donation items or the pile of things you plan to sell sit around your garage or basement for months on end; inevitably someone in your family will start digging through it, and the clutter will be right back where it started. As soon as you've filled a box, put it in your car so you can drop it off at the nearest donation center as soon as you can. Likewise, if you plan to have a garage sale or sell something on Craigslist, do it right away.

- **Work together.** When it comes to clearing clutter once and for all, it is pretty crucial to be on the same page as your spouse. Not only will you accomplish more if you tackle it together or divide and conquer different areas; you will also be motivated by having a partner to cheer you on. If your kids are old enough, get them involved and excited about the process as well. Perhaps even consider letting them keep the money from stuff you sell. Define your battleground as us versus the clutter, and be determined to win!

- **Stop the flow.** For us bargain shoppers especially, this is the step that can be so incredibly hard. The simple fact is that if you truly want to live clutter free, you must *stop buying more stuff.* Commit to doing whatever it takes to stop bringing in more. The biggest cure for me comes from avoiding temptation as much as possible. The truth is that even now if I go to Target or the craft store or the mall, chances are I will find something to buy. I will probably even find multiple somethings. So unless there is something I absolutely, positively, beyond the shadow of a doubt must have, I just don't go. The same goes for thrift stores, garage sales, and online shopping sites. Remember, just because it is a "good deal" doesn't mean you need it. Buying nothing will always be cheaper than buying something on sale.

- **Set strict limits.** We live in a time of more excess and waste than ever before. We think nothing of having a closet full of clothes, when fifty or sixty years ago most women got by with just a few dresses and a single pair of shoes. Holidays and birthdays are accompanied by piles of gifts rather than just one or two, while our kitchens and bathrooms are packed to the gills with gadgets, accessories, and products. In an era when everything is available and, for the most part, affordable, we have to be diligent about setting limits for ourselves. One way I did this was in my bedroom closet, where I limited my clothing to what would fit on forty hangers. Compared to the closets of a century ago, forty hangers is still a lot, but for me — and probably for most women today — it was a pretty drastic change. I purged everything that didn't fit or that I hadn't worn within the last year, and suddenly instead of feeling like I had nothing to wear, I felt like I had stumbled on a whole new wardrobe, one I actually loved!

- **Value quality over quantity.** I think sometimes we have become so accustomed to the steady flow of cheaply made junk that we forget that quality really does matter. At some point our standards lowered so much that we no longer think twice when a blender motor stops working after a year, or when our still-new T-shirt gets a hole after just a few washings, or when yet another cheap toy breaks after being played with for only a week. Being incredibly selective about what you buy — but then spending a little more to purchase something that will stand the test of time — is both frugal and better for the environment. When you do find yourself in need of something new, commit to actively seeking out things made from quality materials. Take the time to read reviews or to find things that are made locally rather than overseas. Choose long-term value over short-term savings.

Taking the Holidays
Down a Notch

After taking my kids' toys away and then sharing that experience on my blog, many people asked what on earth I planned to do about Christmas and birthdays if we weren't giving toys. Though I hadn't thought too much about it ahead of time, hearing this same question so many times made me realize that for many families, these special occasions have truly become all about how much we can get rather than about what we can give.

Although we had always tried, on some level, to make birthdays and holidays more about the experience than the presents, it wasn't until we took the girls' toys away and began actively working together to clear the clutter that Chuck and I realized we needed to make some serious changes. We started by emphasizing to our girls the value of fun family traditions and experiences rather than the gifts. We talked regularly with them about what it means to have an *attitude of gratitude*, and how we can show that gratitude by serving others. We explain that Jesus told us it is the job of people who have been given much to help those who have less, and we actively look for ways to volunteer as a family.

Some of our favorite holiday memories come from those opportunities to serve. Each year we enjoy filling Operation Christmas Child boxes. The girls pick out items for girls their own age, and we spend time talking about where the boxes might go and what life is like for those kids in other countries. On Thanksgiving we spend a few hours delivering meals to elderly shut-ins, and we try to volunteer to ring the

Salvation Army bell outside the local Publix at least a few times each November and December. On Christmas Eve we always deliver cookies to the local fire station to say thank you to those who work to keep us safe while the rest of us are home with our families. That tradition has become our whole family's very favorite part of Christmas!

This is not to say we never give our kids gifts; we do. We just try to limit the quantity and to give things they truly need—such as new clothes or shoes or books—along with perhaps one thing they might want. We also prefer paying for experiences, such as a trip to a theme park or the zoo or going on a family vacation, rather than just getting them another toy.

Changing the attitudes of our friends and family took a little longer, but we found it was possible, even for the auntie whose propensity for going overboard had contributed so heavily to our toy chaos in the first place. The first time we requested no gifts for our daughter's birthday party, not a single person heeded that request. (Though, in fairness, most of the gifts were books and art supplies, not toys.) The next go-round we were a little more adamant and told our friends we would have a donation box at the door and all gifts would automatically be donated. That approach worked like a charm! Family members, realizing we were serious, began asking about what the girls really needed instead of simply buying them anything and everything under the sun.

For us, taking the holidays down a notch also means not always making such a fuss about every occasion that comes along. We make a big deal for birthdays and Thanksgiving and Christmas and Easter, but we don't do much for all the minor holidays, such as Valentine's Day, Halloween, and the Fourth of July.

My children are *not* deprived; on the contrary, compared to most of the world, and even to many children here in the United States, they are ridiculously spoiled. They have two parents who love them deeply. They have a comfortable house to live in, a warm bed to sleep in, clothing to wear, shoes on their feet, clean water to drink, and plenty of food to eat. They have free access to books and art supplies and computers. They go to the dentist and doctor regularly. They get to go to school and ride bikes and swim and play soccer and take dance and gymnastics and violin lessons. They are healthy and happy and blessed beyond measure.

There are many gifts I can give my children, but the gift I *don't* want to give them—or myself, for that matter—is just more stuff. Instead, I want my gift to them to be a life filled with the things that matter most, things like faith, joy, peace, fellowship, contentment, gratitude, and compassion. If living well means having less but appreciating more, then I can't help thinking this is the best gift of all.

CHALLENGE: **Purge Your Excess Stuff**

Take an honest look at the state of your home. Are you drowning in stuff? Are there toys everywhere? Do you feel overrun by clutter? Are your closets, cabinets, and drawers in disarray? Is your basement or attic or garage filled to the brim? How would your life be different if you weren't constantly wrangling with all the excess? How would your children be different if they weren't overwhelmed by so much stuff?

With your spouse and children, make a plan to begin clearing out the excess clutter in your home. Start with the area that bothers you the most, whether it be the kids' rooms, the garage, or perhaps even your kitchen or living area. Get access to free cleaning and organizing checklists at www.livingwellspending less.com/organizingtools, or by using the QR code on this page. Ruthlessly purge  your home of the things you no longer want or need, using the guidelines laid out earlier in this chapter.

Finally, as you begin to declutter, also make a commitment to stop bringing in more stuff. Avoid the stores that tempt you the most, and work at valuing quality over quantity for the things you do need.

PART TWO

Spending Less

We Need to Spend Less Than We Think We Do

We buy things we don't need with money we don't have to impress people we don't like.

Dave Ramsey

"So do not worry, saying 'What shall we eat?' or 'What shall we drink?' or 'What shall we wear?' For the pagans run after all these things, and your heavenly Father knows that you need them. But seek first his kingdom and his righteousness, and all these things will be given to you as well."

Matthew 6:31–33

Abundance isn't God's provision for me to live in luxury. It's his provision for me to help others live. God entrusts me with his money, not to build my kingdom on earth, but to build his kingdom in heaven.

Randy Alcorn

The moment those red-framed sliding glass doors open, my heart starts to pound. My palms get a little sweaty, and my mouth feels dry. From my vantage point in the doorway I can already see the colorful scarf display in the accessory department. *Those are so cute! I should become a scarf person.* Immediately my mind is filled with Becky Bloomwood-esque* visions of bright sweaters topped with colorful scarves paired with skinny jeans and a pair of killer boots. I could be known as *The Girl in the Scarf.* Never mind the fact that I live in South Florida where the temperature only rarely dips below seventy-five degrees.

The tantalizing smell of coffee from the Starbucks on the left snaps me out of my reverie. As I patiently wait for my $5 double-tall-one-and-a-half-pump cinnamon dolce latte, extra hot, I peruse the One Spot area nearby. How handy that they have this little dollar store section right at the entrance! By the time my coffee is ready, my extra-large shiny red cart is piled with cheap trinkets I've already decided I can't live without.

And I'm still standing at the entrance to the store.

It only gets worse from there. I succumb to my new-found scarf obsession and pick up not one but three new

---

* A reference to the main character in the Shopaholic series of books by Sophie Kinsella.

scarves. After all, they are on sale, and besides, I can't be known as *The Girl in the Scarf* if I only ever wear one color, right? But then I realize I don't have any cute sweaters to pair with the scarves, and, as luck would have it, Merona V-Neck sweaters just happen to be 40 percent off in the very next department. Score!

The promotions are calling to me in every aisle, and by the time I get to the girls' clothing section to look at dresses for my oldest daughter — the only thing I actually came in for — my cart is piled high. There are the pretty new containers — 10 percent off this week only — that I just know will finally solve all of my bathroom storage problems. *I will be The Girl with the Organized Bathroom*, I think to myself, captivated by visions of neatly arranged toiletries. There's the new all-purpose cleaner that just seems so much better than the fourteen or so bottles of cleaner I already have at home. This one is organic and smells like Coconut Lime Verbena. I don't actually know what "Verbena" means, but I want it. There's also a selection of Nate Berkus limited edition candles. They smell so good! And they're so cute! And they're only available for a limited time!

I'm already on a roll, so the girls' clothing department is hardly an exercise in self-restraint. There are just so many cute things! *She really does need some new clothes*, I tell myself. *She's growing like a weed*. There are purple velour pants and denim-look jeggings, cowl-neck sweaters and sequin-embellished tees. She's just a little girl but already far more stylish than I could ever hope to be. *I will be The Girl with the Adorable Fashionista Daughter*. Obviously what she wears is a direct reflection of my parenting ability. If she's not well dressed, I must be a terrible mother.

With every item that falls into the cart, I get a new thrill. That euphoric rush of buying one more thing drowns out the voice of reason in the back of my head that says, *Stop! You don't really need any of it. You don't even want this!* Checkout is a blur. All my second thoughts are distracted by the need to strategize my payment options. I pay some with cash, some with debit, then split the remaining balance between two other credit cards. I throw away the receipt on the way out the door, destroying the evidence.

On the drive home I practice justifying my purchases, praying that Chuck won't be home yet so I can distribute the goods before he sees how much I really bought. *We really needed it, honey; we did. Don't worry; it's a gift. We're almost out of this; I needed to get more. But it was on sale!* I might even have to pull out the big guns: *But I got this for you!*

The truth is that I am filled with regret. I know, deep down, that I should turn around and bring it all back, but I don't. The back of my Tahoe is packed to the brim with white plastic bags full of stuff I don't need and can't really afford. We are already drowning in the purchases I've made, and I just bought more. Why can't I stop?

I feel so alone.

But I know I'm not.

A Dangerous Habit

According to a 2012 Rasmussen survey for Country Financial, 52 percent — *more than half* the population — of

Americans spend more than they earn at least a few months out of the year, and 21 percent — one in five — *regularly* have monthly expenses that exceed their income. Interestingly, in that same survey, only 9 percent believe their lifestyle is more than they can afford.[13] Their reasons for overspending included a lack of savings goals, easy access to credit cards, and wanting to feel good or to have a sense of power, as well as wanting to maintain a certain lifestyle or keep up a certain image.[14] Overall it seems our culture of consumerism and instant gratification has become so pervasive that our sense of entitlement has eclipsed our ability to do basic math.

For some, that tendency to overspend crosses over into even more dangerous territory — that of a serious shopping addiction or a compulsive buying disorder, which is "characterized by an obsession with shopping and buying behavior that causes adverse consequences."[15] These adverse consequences can include everything from guilt to excess clutter to marital issues to credit card debt, and, in extreme cases, even financial hardship, home foreclosures, and bankruptcy.

In addition to regularly spending over one's budget, signs of a serious problem include compulsively buying far more than intended; a chronic tendency to shop for shopping's sake; hiding purchases from a spouse or significant other; frequently returning purchases out of guilt; experiencing clear consequences as a result of overspending, such as missing payments or accumulating excessive debt; shopping to alleviate stress or sadness; fighting with one's spouse or significant other about shopping habits; buying most items on credit; feeling a "rush" while spending; feeling guilty or ashamed after a shopping spree; lying about how much money has been spent; justifying purchases ("it was on sale"); and spending time juggling accounts or credit cards to accommodate spending.[16]

According to a 2006 study from the Stanford University School of Medicine, approximately 6 percent of Americans are considered *actual* "shopaholics" (defined by being able to identify with four or more of the behaviors listed above).[17] However, the Rasmussen research on overspending mentioned above indicates that compulsive shopping and overspending are problems for far more than 6 percent of us. Regardless of where we fall on the spectrum, the first step for anyone struggling with a shopping addiction, chronic overspending, financial stress, or credit card debt is admitting there is a problem and realizing it is not okay to spend more than we earn. Nothing will ever get better without our owning the mistakes we've made.

Retail Therapy and Other Lies

While taking personal responsibility for our own spending habits is an essential part of the solution, we must also recognize that a society and culture that glorify mindless spending and encourage instant gratification is a very big part of the problem. We have become a nation of people who spend money on things we don't need, simply because we are bored. Shopping has become a way to pass the time rather than an only-when-necessary means to an end. We pride ourselves on our ability to spot a bargain, to dig through those clearance racks like a champion, even when we're not looking for anything in particular. Spending a Saturday morning perusing the latest One Day Sale (didn't they just have one last week?) is a favorite hobby, while scouting out treasures at garage sales or secondhand stores is practically a sport. We tell ourselves it is a good deal. *It's only a few dollars*, we say. *Besides, this is fun.*

This is hardly an accident. Retailers and advertisers have been more than happy to propagate the idea that bargain hunting and shopping for no apparent reason is a perfectly acceptable pastime, to the point where we will literally rush out of Thanksgiving dinner just to battle the crowds for a chance to buy a $10 toaster or $200 flat-screen TV, even though the toaster and television we already have at home work just fine. Millions of dollars are spent researching every facet of consumer behavior in a not-so-subtle attempt to get us to spend more. This includes everything from creating false hype with "blowout sales" to encouraging excess by providing giant shopping carts or shopping bags to fill, strategically planning store layouts to put the most profitable items in the best spots, purposely making rebates as difficult as possible to redeem, confusing shoppers to make it seem like something is a bargain when it's really not, and taking advantage of impulse shopping.[18] Whether or not we can actually afford it is never an issue; credit cards, layaway options, and payment plans abound.

This myth of shopping as a hobby is so pervasive that women especially are almost made to feel like there is something inherently wrong with them if they don't actually like to shop. Have you ever browsed in the card section of your local Hallmark store and noticed how many birthday cards for women include references to shopping? We have been inundated with slogans, cheers, and mantras to validate a behavior that is inherently destructive: *Shop 'til you drop! If the shoe fits, buy it in every color! Just charge it! Shopping is my cardio. Only X shopping days left until Christmas! It's on sale! It's not shopping; it's retail therapy. I'd rather be shopping! Final clearance!* And the list goes on and on.

The second most important step we can take to improve our financial health — after first admitting that overspending is actually a problem — is to stop this vicious cycle of mindless spending. Shopping without purpose is *not* a fun and innocent way to kill a few hours; it is a destructive behavior that will blow our budget, put us in serious debt, and clutter our lives with stuff we don't really want. Retail therapy is a *myth*, a big fat lie that retailers and credit card companies would love for you to buy into. The scary truth is that spending our hard-earned money on shoes and clothing and gadgets and accessories we don't actually need is the direct *opposite* of therapeutic! At the end of the day, retail therapy ultimately does nothing more than cause additional stress and heartache.

Stewardship Matters

Overspending and mindless shopping can be destructive habits, whether we have a little or a lot. In fact, mindless spending might even be a little easier to keep in check when money is very tight, or at least when credit is not readily available. The real problem comes for those of us with a little more to spend, those of us who have fooled ourselves into thinking we are securely middle-class. We buy into the lies and myths, telling ourselves, *Sure, shopping can be dangerous if you can't afford it. But I can afford it, and it is fun. I've never missed a payment. I've got great credit. Besides, I've earned it, and I deserve to have a little fun. It's my money. Why shouldn't I be able to buy whatever I want, whenever I want?*

Why indeed? As a Christian, I decided I had no choice but to look at the way I spend my money in a different light. The world may be full of ideas about when and where and how much we spend, but the Bible also has a whole lot to say about how we use our money. My favorite lessons are found in the parable of the bags of gold:

> "Again it will be like a man going on a journey, who called his servants and entrusted his wealth to them. To one he gave five bags of gold, to another two bags, and to another one bag, each according to his ability. Then he went on his journey. The man who had received five bags of gold went at once and put his money to work and gained five bags more. So also, the one with two bags of gold gained two more. But the man who had received one bag went off, dug a hole in the ground and hid his master's money.
>
> "After a long time the master of those servants returned and settled accounts with them. The man who had received five bags of gold brought the other five. 'Master,' he said, 'you entrusted me with five bags of gold. See, I have gained five more.'
>
> "His master replied, 'Well done, good and faithful servant! You have been faithful with a few things; I will put you in charge of many things. Come and share your master's happiness!'

"The man with two bags of gold also came. 'Master,' he said, 'you entrusted me with two bags of gold; see, I have gained two more.'

"His master replied, 'Well done, good and faithful servant! You have been faithful with a few things; I will put you in charge of many things. Come and share your master's happiness!'

"Then the man who had received one bag of gold came. 'Master,' he said, 'I knew that you are a hard man, harvesting where you have not sown and gathering where you have not scattered seed. So I was afraid and went out and hid your gold in the ground. See, here is what belongs to you.'

"His master replied, 'You wicked, lazy servant! So you knew that I harvest where I have not sown and gather where I have not scattered seed? Well then, you should have put my money on deposit with the bankers, so that when I returned I would have received it back with interest.

"'So take the bag of gold from him and give it to the one who has ten bags. For whoever who has will be given more, and they will have an abundance. Whoever does not have, even what they have will be taken from them. And throw that worthless servant outside, into the darkness, where there will be weeping and gnashing of teeth.'"

MATTHEW 25:14–30

This simple parable tells us pretty much everything we need to know about the importance of good stewardship. How we spend our money matters a lot to God. We aren't simply advised to use our money wisely; we are called, in no uncertain terms, to be good stewards of the resources we have been given, regardless of how much we have. Our money is not our own.

In the parable of the bags of gold, the master expected his servants not to hoard or squander his money, but rather to use it wisely, taking calculated risks and making investments that would grow his wealth. He expected them to work hard, to put off immediate gratification for the promise of a bigger reward down the line. He gave each of his servants a different amount, based on their abilities, but he gave each of them *something*. He knew they all had the potential to make good decisions with the money, and he was angry at the servant with one bag of gold, not because he failed to use the money wisely, but because *he didn't even try*.

Luke 16:10–12 tells us, "Whoever can be trusted with very little can also be trusted with much, and whoever is dishonest with very little will also be dishonest with much. So if you have not been trustworthy in handling worldly wealth, who will trust you with true riches? And if you have not been trustworthy with someone else's property, who will give you property of your own?"

With many blessings comes much responsibility. As we've already discussed, simply being born into a country with access to education and health care and transportation, and living in a home with electricity and heat and running water, puts us, regardless of income, in the top stratum of the world's population. Poverty in the United States looks a whole lot like wealth in other countries. Buying whatever we want when we want it, spending on credit when we can't afford it, and trying to keep up with the Joneses just because it seems like the thing to do are not signs of being good stewards of God's money. While popular culture would have us believe our spending is all about us, the truth is that what we spend is really all about *God*.

Are you using the resources you have been given to the very best of your ability? Have you handled your worldly wealth with wisdom and discernment? Are you being trustworthy with God's money?

A Month of Zero Spending

When I started writing my blog, *Living Well Spending Less*, in 2010, it wasn't because I was some slick money guru or finance major who wanted to pass on my certified wisdom to the world. Far from it, actually. I started writing a blog because my spending was out of control and my marriage was on the brink of both divorce and financial ruin. I started my blog to save my marriage, my family, and myself. My goal in the beginning was simply to learn how to stretch my budget so I could still buy all the things I wanted. And there was *so much* I wanted! I became good—great, even—at finding the best deals and discounts on groceries, clothing, and other household goods. But I was still *spending*, not saving.

It was my husband, Chuck, who first suggested we try a spending freeze. He had discovered in the backseat a bag of clothes I had recently purchased at Anthropologie. If you've ever shopped there, you know the clothes can be a little pricey, but, being a "thrifty" shopper, I of course headed straight to the sale room and found four darling tops I was quite sure I couldn't live without for a whopping *75 percent off*. Yes, 75 percent off! At Anthropologie! Friends, these kinds of sales don't just happen every day! It was practically a no-brainer. *Of course* I had to buy them. It was an amazing deal! A bargain! I was literally saving *hundreds* of dollars! Right?

Chuck didn't *quite* see it that way. He pointed out, perhaps not as lovingly as he could have, that in reality I hadn't *saved* anything. I had spent $150 to fill a closet that was already full. Chagrined, I agreed to a month of zero spending.

To be honest, I wasn't totally sure I could do it. Thirty-one days of spending *nothing*? No fancy lattes, no eating out, no trips to Target? Or even the craft store? The prospect was daunting, but our rule was simple: Cut out all nonessential spending for one month. This meant we could still pay our normal bills and buy a few perishable food items such as milk, bread, and vegetables. Everything else was off-limits.

I could never have predicted the profound change a month of zero spending would have on our family. I am not exaggerating when I say it was one of the best things we have ever done. Our intent was to save money—which we did, to the tune of a little more than $1,000 in just thirty days—but what we got out of the experience was so much more than a bigger bank account.

I'm not going to lie; there were some tough moments in that first month of no spending. Three days into our challenge I was *really* regretting my lack of foresight to stock up on ice cream (granted, that would have been *cheating*), and about halfway through the month I may or may not have willingly traded one of my children for a Starbucks gift card.

We ate more than a few very random—or *creative*, as we liked to tell the kids—meals, and as we choked them down, we sometimes found ourselves longingly reminiscing about our favorite meals at our favorite restaurants. My girls began counting the days until we could go back to the all-you-can-eat buffet at the Golden Corral. (Yep, we really know how to live!)

Even so, freezing our spending forced us to look at our life differently. The challenge forced us to pay attention to the things we already had right in front of us, instead of constantly looking to get something new. It gave us a built-in excuse to say no to all the activities and distractions that are constantly vying for our attention. We spent more time together as a family, fought less, shared more, and became far more creative. We cleared out most of the long-forgotten food in our pantry and freezer, and we tackled some hard money discussions we had previously avoided. It was also a great lesson for our daughters. One morning, about halfway through the month, I overheard my oldest daughter explaining to her sister that we couldn't buy more Life Savers to fill our candy bowl because candy was a "want" and not a "need." I knew then that they got it.

As much as I would like to say I've got this whole financial expert thing nailed down, I'm almost sure there will always be a part of me that is addicted to shopping. I am constantly tempted to make poor money decisions, and the reality is that my most recent trip to Target didn't look all that different from the one described at the beginning of this chapter. I had gone in for just a few things—items we really *did* need—and, just like old times, came home with a Tahoe full of bull's-eye-dotted white bags. As I walked in, guilt written all over my face, my husband just shook his head, put his arm around me, and laughed. *Oh, honey, you know you're never allowed to go shopping at Target ever again, right?*

Once I've gotten into "spend mode," it can be hard to stop, even when I know I need to. When this happens, I've found the very best thing I can do to turn things around quickly is to commit to another month of zero spending. It is almost like pressing the reset button on my brain. Thankfully, those momentary relapses now happen rarely enough that we can laugh about it, return the excess, and move on.

In our consumer-driven culture, the pressure to spend and keep spending — even to the point of our own financial demise — is intense. We are bombarded with messages telling us that if we don't have the newest iPhone or the biggest flat-screen or the nicest minivan or even the latest styles from Anthropologie, we will be missing something important. The reality is that stuff does not bring happiness. Instead, buying more than we need breeds nothing but discontentment. Don't fall for the hype. Take a month off. It just might change your life.

CHALLENGE: **Freeze Your Spending**

Commit to a month of ZERO spending on anything but the barest of essentials. This means no new clothes, gadgets, home improvements, craft projects, and *especially* no eating at restaurants. It means staying home instead of going out. It means buying as few perishable grocery items as possible, and instead eating the long-forgotten items in your pantry and freezer. For one month, your goal will be to simply use what you have.

For moral support, daily challenges, and printable worksheets, you can access the 31 Days of Living Well & Spending Zero challenge at LivingWellSpendingLess.com.  You can find it at www.living wellspendingless.com/lwsz or by scanning the QR code on this page.

Saving Is a State of Mind

A man is rich in proportion to the number of things he can afford to leave alone.

Henry David Thoreau

A good person leaves an inheritance for their children's children,
   but a sinner's wealth is stored up for the righteous.

Proverbs 13:22

The quickest way to double your money is to fold it in half and put it in your back pocket.

Will Rogers

Some of us are born to shop while others are destined to save every penny. As you've probably already figured out, there has never really been a question as to which category I fall into. For as long as I can remember, money has burned a hole in my pocket. Every allowance was gone by the end of the day; every dollar earned babysitting or doing yard work or selling lemonade was gone before I even knew what to do with it. The second that cash was in my hand, I was off on my bicycle to Sprouse-Reitz, the local five-and-dime store, eager to buy whatever treasure happened to catch my eye. Sometimes it was craft supplies, sometimes toys, sometimes just candy. It never much mattered what I bought; all I knew was that I had to buy *something*.

As I was growing up, the first and only rule of money in my family was that we didn't talk about money. Ever. Anytime I asked how much we had — or whether we were rich, as the kids at school sometimes said — my parents' only response was, *We don't talk about money.* All I ever knew is that we had more than enough. The bills were paid. There was plenty of food on the table, clothes in our closets, a pile of presents under the Christmas tree. We went on exotic family vacations to places like Mexico and Hawaii and even to Europe; we had a housekeeper who cleaned our house three times a week; and there was a pool and a tennis court in our backyard.

In high school I discovered the convenience of using my parents' credit cards—sometimes with permission and sometimes without—and shopped without restraint. They never seemed to notice what I bought, and the bills were always paid. Although I was eager to earn money of my own, and even though I worked hard at everything from cleaning hotel rooms to picking strawberries to babysitting every child in our neighborhood, I really had zero concept of the actual value of money. When I went off to college, my dad cosigned my first credit card, which I managed to max out in the first semester, even as I worked full-time. My dad, trying to be nice rather than seizing the opportunity to teach me a serious lesson, just paid off the entire bill without saying a word. Not surprisingly, I learned nothing. The card was maxed out again just a few months later.

I spent because I could. It was easy, and it was all I knew. My good credit on that first card resulted in many more approvals on credit cards my dad *wasn't* responsible for. By my senior year of college, I was unhappily married, severely depressed, and up to my eyeballs in credit card bills. Eventually my world crumbled completely, and my dire financial situation took a backseat to the dark world of depression. When I finally started to recover, I found myself divorced, deeply in debt, and utterly alone. According to my attorney, I had little choice but to file for bankruptcy.

Starting over with nothing was scary, but I was determined not to screw it up. I got a job and a little apartment and paid cash for everything. For a long time I didn't even have a bank account—my credit was so bad that no bank would have me. I still spent every penny I earned, but I figured at least I was self-sufficient and not in debt, which for me was a vast improvement over any other stage of my adult life.

And then, a few years into this frugal-by-necessity, cash-only lifestyle, I met Chuck, who was smart, successful, and far more money savvy than I could ever hope to be. He was the consummate saver, the one who had always done everything right when it came to money. He was wise about putting money away in Roth IRAs and 401(k)s, knew how to make smart investments, and understood all that crazy Wall Street terminology that still makes my head spin. He had spent his whole life working hard and making good financial decisions.

And suddenly I didn't have to be so careful anymore.

You've already heard what happened next: I reverted right back into my old shopaholic ways, eroding the financial security my husband had worked his whole life to create. Eventually my spending became totally out of control and threatened to destroy my marriage, until I agreed to a strict allowance and started a blog called *Living Well Spending Less* to hold myself accountable.

My only goal at first was simply to figure out how to stretch my budget so I could still buy all the things I wanted. There was so much I still wanted, so many pretty things out there just waiting for me to take them home. While I became quite good at getting discounts — really good discounts — on groceries, clothing, and other household goods, I was still spending, not saving.

But a funny thing happened along the way. The more I pursued a truly frugal lifestyle and, more importantly, the more fervently I prayed for God to change my heart and to take away my desire for the things of this world, the *less I wanted*. Suddenly the discounts didn't matter quite so much. I realized I was drowning in things I didn't need or even want. I began to crave and seek not just financial freedom or financial security, but true financial *peace*.

Learning to budget and save, to make wise financial decisions and to live within our means are critical and very necessary skills. No other facet of our life is as all-encompassing as money; it literally affects every single thing we do. And make no mistake; learning and mastering these skills is *hard work*. But for those of us who struggle daily with that urge to spend, for those of us who lack discipline and self-restraint, the process of saving must be much more than the act of putting money in the right columns on a spreadsheet. We must *first* let God change our hearts.

The word *peace* is defined in the dictionary as "a state in which there is no war or fighting; a state of tranquility or freedom from disquieting or oppressive thoughts or emotions; harmony in personal relations; contentment."

Financial peace, therefore, can be defined as "a state of mutual harmony with money; freedom from oppressive thoughts or emotions related to spending; harmony in personal relationships and freedom from strife or dissension regarding personal finances; contentment with what one has." Financial peace is not a number on our bank statement or a perfectly balanced budget; it is instead a *state of mind*. There will never be enough money or pretty things to satisfy our broken, discontented hearts, but praying for peace with where we are and what we have *right now* will mean instant wealth far greater than anything the world has to offer.

Financial freedom and financial peace go hand in hand, but while one comes from hard work and discipline, the other can only come from above. We need both to succeed.

Creating a Budget

While financial *peace* starts with prayer and a change in our heart, financial *freedom* starts with creating—and sticking to—a realistic budget. When we know we've been spending too much, just the idea of creating a budget can seem incredibly scary. The mere thought of taking an honest look at one's current financial state is enough for many of us to break out in a cold sweat. In fact, according to a recent Gallup poll, only 32 percent of Americans—just one in three—actually prepare a detailed budget each month, and only 24 percent have a long-term financial plan.[19] It is so much easier to justify all those not-so-necessary expenditures when we don't actually know how much we're spending, or how it relates to how much income we are bringing in. We tell ourselves that ignorance is bliss. This is, of course, just one *more* big fat lie.

Setting up and sticking to a budget might seem scary and overwhelming at first, but the truth is that not having a clear picture of one's financial state is a much scarier prospect. The ongoing stress of never quite knowing whether the next check will clear, or whether there will be enough money to make the mortgage payment, is far worse than a few hours spent being honest with yourself. No matter how out of control your financial state may be, taking the time to make a plan for the future will always be better than burying your head in the sand. And take it from someone who has been there, facing your fears is the most freeing thing you might ever do. The instant you have finished that first budget, you will feel like the weight of the world has been lifted off your shoulders.

The system you use to create your budget is up to you. After completing Dave Ramsey's Financial Peace University class, my husband and I began using Dave's monthly cash flow plan, which you can download for free at DaveRamsey.com. He also has a quick-start budget available, which provides a great place to begin, especially if you are feeling overwhelmed. Both Financial Peace University and Dave Ramsey's book *The Total Money Makeover* are excellent resources for figuring out a budget and making a plan to get out of debt. I cannot recommend either of them strongly enough! Other options for budgeting include online software found at YouNeedaBudget.com or Mint.com. I also have free printable budgeting worksheets available on Living WellSpendingLess.com, which can be found at www.living wellspendingless.com/budgetworksheet/.

Regardless of which budgeting system you decide to use, the process is the same, and if you are married, this is one of those things that really must be done together. A family budget will never work unless you are both an integral part of creating it. The first step is to start by identifying your income. Unless you have mysterious streams of money flowing in from sources unknown (wouldn't that be nice?), this part should be pretty easy. In addition to your regular salary, be sure to include income from rental properties, investment dividends, or child support, if applicable. If your income is irregular, there are a couple of options. You can base your budget on a monthly average, or you can base your budget on your typically lowest-income month and then apply the extra from other months into savings.

The next step is determining all of your fixed expenses. These are the things that have to be paid each month, regardless of whether you want to or not—like your mortgage or rent payment, car payments, and insurance, as well as utilities such as gas, electricity, water, waste disposal, phone, Internet, and cable. Be sure to look at your bank statement or copies of recent bills to get an accurate idea of what you are actually paying for all these things and to make sure you don't forget anything. Your fixed expenses should also include any money you want to set aside each month for charitable giving or tithing and for saving, because if you don't set money aside for these things *first*, chances are there won't be any left at the end of the month. Finally, add up the total of your fixed expenses and subtract this number from your income; the number left over will determine how much you have to work with for your variable expenses.

The third step, then, is to figure out what all those variable expenses are and how much you can afford to spend on them. This includes *everything else*, from food and gas to entertainment, clothing, car and home repair, and eating out. My husband and I found it most helpful to make a list on a separate piece of paper of all the things that we could think of that we spend money on, as well as how much we estimated we spent on each item. It was when we added up the total of *that* list that we realized how much we really needed to cut back! With a number to start with, we worked backward, deciding what we could eliminate and cut back on, until the total of our variable expenses matched the amount we actually had available to spend.

Saving on the Necessary Stuff

After spending time sorting out your budget, tracking your expenses, and figuring out exactly how much you have to spend, you may come to the realization that it is time to get serious about saving wherever and however you can. Most expenses can be broadly categorized into two areas—that which we *must* spend money on, and that which we *want* to spend money on. Obviously the first things that need to get cut when money is tight are the wants and not the needs, but it sure is nice to save on the necessary so there is more left over for the fun.

I think the most important thing to keep in mind when it comes to the money we spend is this: *Everything is negotiable.*

We live in a country where, for the most part, companies have to compete for your business. In fact, there are antitrust laws that prevent companies from becoming too large or too powerful. This is something these companies don't really want you to figure out. They would much rather have you believe they are doing you a favor by financing your home or car, or by providing your insurance, because if you believe that, you'll pay whatever they tell you to. These companies know your ignorance means more profit for them, so they will continue feeding you those lies for as long as they can get away with it. But the truth is that they *need* your business. And chances are that if they are not willing to negotiate, some other company out there will. Knowledge is power; use it to your advantage.

When it comes to saving money on your housing costs, a lot of factors will come into play. Do you own or rent? Do you have children and need to be concerned about the school system? How long is your commute? What are the renovation or upkeep costs of your home? Your individual situation will determine your course of action, but in general your goal should be to spend as little as possible on your housing. For renters, this may mean negotiating a new lease or finding roommates. Meanwhile, homeowners might look into refinancing or negotiating with their lender to get a better interest rate. A drastic but sometimes necessary step is to move, downsizing your home or apartment to something more affordable.

Another tough pill to swallow is the idea of minimizing transportation costs. Anyone who has listened to Dave Ramsey's radio show knows that his first piece of advice for anyone trying to get out of debt is "SELL THE CAR!" He loves pointing out the foolishness of someone who is struggling to make ends meet driving around in a brand-new vehicle they can't really afford. Yes, we all want to look good driving around town, but at what expense (and who really sees you behind the glass anyway)? Is the idea of impressing our friends and neighbors worth being saddled with thousands of dollars in debt? Car payments don't *have* to be a part of life, nor should they be. If your budget needs help, one of your first tweaks should be to downgrade your vehicle to one you can buy with cash, or even to pare down to one family vehicle for a while, if necessary. An added benefit to driving an older vehicle is lower insurance costs, but be sure to budget at least $1,000 per year for car repair costs. If that sounds like a lot, remind yourself that you are saving that amount, and then some, in interest and insurance costs on a new vehicle.

A third large and necessary expense that can often be greatly reduced is insurance costs. Between homeowner insurance, auto insurance, health insurance, and life insurance, there is a lot of room for negotiation. Finding the best rates requires some due diligence and willingness to do research and make a lot of phone calls, but the difference can save up to hundreds of dollars each month.

Utilities, gas, and food costs are other common expenses that can't be avoided. Fortunately, most of these can be cut way down as well. In the next chapter we will talk extensively about specific ways to cut your grocery bill in half, but cutting back on utility expenses is often a matter of being more careful and intentional about the resources we often consume without thinking. It means turning off the lights, turning up the temperature on the air conditioner, and turning down the heat in order to cut down on our electricity and gas bills. It means purposely using less water, getting rid of cable TV or a landline, or downgrading our cell phone plan. It can even mean going fewer places or choosing to carpool or use public transit to save on gas.

So much of our spending happens on autopilot that it is quite shocking to realize how many possibilities exist for cutting back, even on those things we need. Delve a little deeper into your own fixed expenses; you may be surprised at what you will find.

Saving on the Fun Stuff

It's 8:45 p.m. at the outlet mall, and the stores will be closing very soon. Today's objective? New shoes for the girls and maybe, just maybe, a new pair of boots for myself. After an hour of shopping, the girls are all set, but the boots I am dreaming about seem to be in short supply. I wander into Nordstrom Rack feeling slightly discouraged, and there they are—the most beautiful pair of hand-embroidered brown suede Old Gringo riding boots I have ever seen, and they just happen to be in my size. I've dreamt about owning a pair of these for years, but the $500+ price tag has always held me back. I longingly stroke the soft suede, already knowing they will be out of my price range. Then, partially for fun and partially to torture myself, I turn one over, just to see.

$54.99.

I blink and do a double take. It must be some sort of mistake. These kinds of boots don't go on sale, and certainly not for a tenth of the normal price. I look around, not daring to believe what I see. Only a fool would pass by a deal like this!

While that exact scenario has happened only in my dreams, there have been more real-life deals that were "too good to pass up" than I can possibly count. I can spot a bargain from a mile away, and when it comes to saving money, the idea of finding a killer pair of boots on clearance for 90 percent off is far, far more exciting to me than the idea of negotiating a better insurance rate or lowering the interest rate on my thirty-year mortgage. After all, both are saving me some serious money, right? What's so wrong about wanting to look good at the same time?

The distinction, of course, is that lowering my mortgage

and insurance payments represents *actual* savings, ones that result in more money in my pocket, while scoring an amazing deal on boots is still really just *spending*. It doesn't matter how good a deal it is if I can't afford it. The whole point of creating a budget is to figure out what you *can* afford so there is room for the fun stuff when you really want it. Telling your money where to go doesn't necessarily mean eliminating every nonessential purchase; it just means making a plan for those purchases that still allows you to meet all your other financial goals as well. That way, when the perfect deal really does come along, you'll be able to snatch it up guilt-free.

Delayed gratification is probably the single best way to save on all those variable and extraneous expenses. I've learned the hard way that impulse buys will kill a budget every single time. Everything goes on sale eventually; getting the very best price is often just a matter of being patient. If there is something you really want—whether it's a family vacation, a new television, or a pair of killer boots—save up for it or set money aside in your budget, and *then*, once the money is already there, start shopping for that amazing deal you know is out there. Then the rest of your dream scenario will look something like this:

Thankfully, I've already set aside $75 in my budget for a moment like this. These boots were meant to be. I do a little happy dance, pay for my boots, and treat myself to a Frappuccino with the extra cash. When I get back home, I grab my bag and run into the house, calling out with pride, "Honey, you'll never guess what I got!"

Saving for the Future

The Future. Big. Undefined. Nonimmediate. Nebulous. Scary. If you're anything like me, saving for this vague entity known as "the future" is the hardest part of all. After all, food, clothing, vacations, housing, and yes, even boots are all real. They are tangible and immediate. Saving for those types of things affects us right now. On the other hand, saving for far-off things, like retirement or college or putting money aside for an emergency fund, is a lot harder, especially when money is tight. It is so much easier to look at the here and now rather than to focus on the big picture. But whether or not it feels real at the moment, that future will eventually catch up to us.

Perhaps your kids, like mine, are still young, and college seems far away. You can barely even imagine them going off to middle school, much less leaving the nest. But time flies, and as much as I'd like to say it won't happen, they will be grown before we know it. While it might not be possible to foot the entire bill, when the time comes for our children to head off to college, wouldn't it be nice to have something to give them?

Retirement is an even scarier prospect, albeit one that is very hard to imagine for those of us in our twenties and thirties. By now we've all heard the scary statistics on how Social Security is on the verge of bankruptcy, and how there is no guarantee that anyone paying into the system now will ever see anything out of it. Do you really want to take the risk of having *nothing* when you enter your golden years?

And then there's the emergencies—those unplanned,

expensive crises that none of us want to think about. Our roof starts leaking and needs to be replaced; the refrigerator stops working; or we have to unexpectedly fly across the country to help a friend in need. Or, in even more serious scenarios, we lose our job, get sick, or experience a natural disaster. As much as we want to hope these type of things won't happen to us, we all know tragedy can strike at any moment. Emergencies are stressful enough as it is, but wondering where we will get the money to pay for them is even worse.

Setting aside money for the future is not a luxury; it is a necessity. And the first line item in every budget should be *savings*, first for a fully funded emergency fund that can provide three to six months' worth of income, and then for college and retirement. While it may not be fun or glamorous to set money aside for the future, and while it may even mean cutting back and pinching pennies in other areas, trust me when I tell you that the peace of mind that comes from having a cushion to fall back on, a buffer against financial uncertainty, is well worth any short-term sacrifices you have to make.

A famous saying often attributed to Augustine goes like this: "Pray as though everything depends on God; work as though everything depends on you"—and these words are never more applicable than when it comes to creating a budget and taking charge of your finances. Discovering true financial peace is, without a doubt, a life-changing experience. Making your money work *for* you instead of against you is quite possibly the most empowering thing you will ever do. It requires hard work and discipline and, most of all, a willingness to forgo instant gratification for long-term gains. It means making a plan and being willing to correct the mistakes you've already made. Most importantly, it means spending time in prayer, asking God to change your heart.

CHALLENGE: Establish a Family Budget

If you are married, make a date with your spouse to sit down and do an honest assessment of your current financial situation. Without blame or anger, try to talk openly and honestly about any struggles you are having. Agree to work together to establish a plan that works for your family. Granted, this is much easier said than done, especially when finances have been a source of struggle in your marriage. For my husband and me, it took attending a finance course for couples held at our church. The same course—Dave Ramsey's Financial Peace University—is offered all over the country. Check out www.FPU.com to find one in your area.

If you don't currently have a monthly budget, spend some time creating one, using one or more of the budgeting resources found at www.livingwellspendingless.com/budgetworksheet, or scan the QR code on this page. Start by

---

identifying your income. Then determine your fixed expenses and set a monthly savings goal. Finally, figure out what you have left to spend on your remaining categories and decide together where to cut back.

Once you've created your first month's budget, start looking at ways to cut your expenses even more by reducing rent or mortgage payments, car payments, insurance rates, and utility expenses. Finally, commit to buying only the things you have budgeted for.

How to Cut Your Grocery Bill in Half

A penny saved is a penny earned.

Benjamin Franklin

The plans of the diligent lead to profit
as surely as haste leads to poverty.

Proverbs 21:5

A bargain ain't a bargain if it is not
something you need.

Sidney Carroll

et's face it; food is expensive. Recently, the USDA estimated that the average family of four would need to spend anywhere from $553 to $1,259 per month on groceries if they ate food prepared at home every day.[20] In recent years, average wages have not increased significantly, but the price of food keeps going up. When you are just trying to feed your family, that trend becomes a definite threat!

Over the past few years, news programs and television shows, like TLC's *Extreme Couponing*, have called a lot of attention to the idea of using coupons to save big money on groceries. If you've ever watched one of these programs, you probably already know the savings can be quite dramatic. The problem is that these dramatic savings often apply to seasoned coupon users who spend countless hours clipping coupons and searching for the very best deals.

Quite frankly, who has time for that on a regular basis? For the average mom or dad who is trying to save on groceries, the idea of exerting all that time and energy on a single shopping trip is not only overwhelming; it is unrealistic. Even so, it *is* possible to cut your grocery bill in half without spending all your time clipping coupons! In fact, even if you never clip a single coupon, you can still save significant money on your grocery bill just by changing the way you shop.

Shop the Sales

There is a little-known secret to saving serious money on groceries that the food companies and grocery store chains don't want you to know. Are you ready for it? The secret is that *extreme grocery savings do not come from coupons*. You don't have to become an extreme couponer in order to save big on groceries, nor do you have to fill your cart with unhealthy processed prepackaged meals and junk food. Furthermore, you can still save on groceries, even if your family eats only organic or gluten-free. No matter who you are or what type of food you prefer to buy, you can spend less by following one simple trick—*shop the sales*.

If you are going to save big on your groceries, the bulk of your savings will always come from the store's sales. The better the promotion, the bigger the savings, so the first step in saving money on your grocery bill is to, as much as possible, shop the sales. Always, always, always buy food when it is at its lowest possible price—otherwise known as the rock-bottom price, which is generally 30 to 50 percent off the everyday price in a normal (nondiscounted) grocery store.

Compare the store sale ads in your area to find out which stores have the best sale prices. Don't assume you know which store has the best deals until you've actually checked; you may be surprised at what you find. While traditional grocery chains often have the highest prices overall, they also usually have the best sales, particularly on name-brand items. For basic, generic food items, discount stores such as Aldi, Save-A-Lot, or even Trader Joe's or Walmart often have everyday lower prices with quality similar to name brands. However, even discount stores sell a lot of items that are marked up. The trick is often not just to know which items to buy at which store, but also to be able to spot a fantastic price when you see it.

The best way to make sure you are always buying your food at its lowest possible price is to maintain an ongoing "rock-bottom price list" to keep track of the best prices for all the items you buy. Don't worry; this sounds a lot harder than it actually is! You can get a free printable rock-bottom price list at *LivingWellSpendingLess.com* that includes both

 my own rock-bottom prices and a blank sheet to keep track of your own. Go to www.livingwellspendingless.com/pricelist or scan the QR code on this page. (It is important to keep in mind that food prices vary a lot by region, so *my* lowest prices for Southwest Florida could look very different from the rock-bottom prices available in New York—or Michigan or Texas or Montana.) You can also dedicate a small, blank notebook to keeping track of prices, or if you prefer digital data, you can create a simple spreadsheet. Whichever method you use, your lowest price list should include categories for all types of food you buy, as well as for the best price you have found for each particular item.

After you've started paying attention to sale prices for a few weeks, you may be surprised at how the rock-bottom prices will immediately begin to jump out at you as you wander through the grocery aisles. Impulse buys become a lot less tempting when you know the very item you are tempted

by was half off just last week. You may also start to notice a pattern in sale prices and even begin to see that most items in the grocery store, with the exception of a few seasonal items, follow a six-to-eight-week sale cycle, which means that if it is on sale now, it will be on sale again in about two months.

Stockpile, Stockpile, Stockpile

Understanding this sale cycle is the second key component of learning how to cut your grocery bill in half. If our goal is to only ever buy items when they are on sale or at their rock-bottom price, we must also learn how to buy enough of a particular item while it is on sale to last until it goes on sale again. This is key. If most items go on sale every eight weeks, then you will need to buy enough while it is on sale to last your family eight weeks. If you only buy a week's worth, you will be forced to pay full price the next time you shop because you didn't buy enough.

For example, say your kids love Honey Nut Cheerios and want to eat a bowl of it for breakfast every single day, which means your family goes through approximately two boxes of cereal every week. The regular price at your grocery store for Honey Nut Cheerios is $4.50 a box, and you normally pick up two boxes on your weekly trip to the grocery store. This week, however, you see that Honey Nut Cheerios are on sale for $1.99, more than half off the regular price! Instead of buying just two boxes like you normally would, you buy twelve boxes, enough to last your family for the six weeks it will take for their favorite cereal to go on sale again.

At first it may seem counterintuitive to buy more instead of less. After all, instead of spending $9.00 on cereal that week, you would be spending $23.88. However, over the course of six weeks you are actually saving $30.12, because the next five times you go to the grocery store you won't have to buy any cereal. It is a very small adjustment, but this one simple change on just one single item would save your family $160 over the course of one year. Imagine how much your family could save if you made this adjustment on all the food you buy!

It does take time to build up a stockpile—usually anywhere from one to three months to establish a good variety of the foods your family eats. Your goal is build up your own mini grocery store that you can then use to plan your family's meals. You will probably find that, while you are buying a larger quantity of food than you normally would, you are actually spending less money on food than ever before.

Despite what you may have seen on television, a well-varied stockpile does not need to take up a whole room in your house, and you do not need to accumulate a whole year's worth of food. Because sale cycles generally run about six to eight weeks, your stockpile should contain about six to eight weeks' worth of a nice variety of food.

While most items follow this six-to-eight-week pattern, there are a few seasonal items that tend to go on sale only once or twice a year. For instance, baking staples such as flour, sugar, and chocolate chips usually go on sale only in the months of November and December, which makes it smart to stock up on a year's worth of those items instead of just six weeks' worth. Likewise, canned soup tends to go on sale only during the winter months; oatmeal tends to go on sale only in January; and lunch bag staples like peanut butter and fruit snacks tend to go on sale at back-to-school time.

If keeping track of sales patterns sounds like too much work, shop at German-owned Aldi, which is quickly becoming the go-to shop of frugal foodies everywhere. There the prices on basic grocery staples are consistently lower than the local grocery store, with comparable — or even better — quality. Once you get used to its quirks — you have to bring a quarter for your grocery cart, provide your own bags, and do your own bagging of groceries — you'll appreciate its streamlined, quick, and inexpensive shopping experience.

Save on Meat and Vegetables

One of the most common complaints I hear about using coupons and saving money on groceries is that the only real "deals" tend to be for unhealthy processed and packaged foods rather than for healthier items like meat, dairy, and fresh produce. True, most manufacturers' coupons are limited to packaged foods, and at first glance it might seem like the only way to cut your grocery bill in half is to resign yourself to a diet of flavored rice, cold cereal, and powdered mashed potatoes. Luckily for all of us, this is not the case! It is possible to maintain a healthy balanced diet and still see significant savings in the checkout line.

Although many meat eaters are reluctant to take this step, the truth is that going vegetarian just twice a week can save a family of four as much as $1,000 a year. Meat — even meat purchased at a discount — is expensive. It is, hands down, the single biggest expense on most people's grocery bill, which means that the simplest way to slash your grocery bill is to *eat less meat.*

I promise that this sounds much more painful than it is! I have personally been a vegetarian for almost twenty years, but my husband and daughters love meat of all kinds. Over the years I've learned to prepare hearty meat-free meals that can satisfy all of our very different tastes. Some of our favorite meat-free meals include a wide variety of vegetarian soups and chili, vegetable frittata or quiche, spaghetti or other pasta dishes, eggplant parmesan, or even a jazzed-up version of beans and rice. I will often substitute vegetarian crumbles for ground beef in recipes such as tacos, meatloaf, or shepherd's pie. These crumbles are found next to the veggie burgers in the freezer section and can often be purchased on sale with a coupon for less than a dollar per bag.

Then, when you *do* decide to buy and cook with meat, use the following strategies to keep your costs down:

- **Buy in bulk.** In general, the larger the quantity, the cheaper the price per pound. Take advantage of the economy-priced family-size packages; then freeze the excess. Other creative options for bulk meat purchases include teaming up with a few other families to purchase an entire cow, then splitting the meat. (Contact a local independent butcher or meat vendor for more information.) Zaycon Foods (www .ZayconFoods.com) also offers high-quality meat in bulk at special events around the country.

- **Make it stretch.** Cook with meat in smaller quantities and make it go farther by adding bread crumbs or beans to your ground beef. Soups and casseroles can generally get away with less meat than the recipe calls for as well.

- **Look for discounts.** By now it should go without saying that meat should only be purchased when it is on sale, but in addition to their regular sale prices, many grocery stores will discount meat at the end of the day in order to get rid of it quickly. Take advantage of these rock-bottom prices; then freeze the meat to use when you need it. In addition, discount grocery stores such as Aldi or Save-A-Lot often have great prices on meat!

- **Skip convenience.** Keep in mind that the more "ready to eat" the meat, the more expensive it will typically be. Buying simple cuts that require your own trimming and prep work can mean big savings at the checkout stand, as will grinding your own meat (or purchasing a chuck roast and asking the butcher to grind it for you). Furthermore, buying cheaper cuts of meats that require longer cooking times or additional tenderizing is a much thriftier option than splurging on prime cuts.

Of course, a cart full of fresh produce can blow your grocery budget almost as quickly as one full of meat, so it is just as important to save on fruits and vegetables as it is on meat. Here are some of my favorite tips for saving on produce:

- **Shop in season.** Produce will always be cheapest when it is in season, which means your shopping habits should follow suit. Don't buy blueberries in January or Brussels sprouts in July. Instead, pay attention to growing seasons in order to get the best price and quality. You can find a printable seasonal produce chart  at www.livingwellspendingless.com/producechart, or scan the QR code on this page, to keep track of what fruits and vegetables to purchase when. Or just check your local grocery store's flyer or website to see what's on sale that week.

- **Price match.** A little effort in research can pay off big-time if you have a lot of produce to buy. Spend a few minutes finding all the best prices in each local grocery store's sale flyers, then take advantage of Walmart's (or other grocery stores') price match policy and get all your produce in one place for the lowest possible price.

- **Stay local.** Skip the marked-up prices at your grocery store and instead go straight to the source. Roadside stands and farmer's markets can be great places to score the freshest produce at great prices. Don't be afraid to barter for a discount, and show up right before close to get an even better price. Another great option is to participate in a local farm membership co-op, which will give you a weekly selection of vegetables for an entire growing season. Check out www.localharvest.org to find a co-op in your area.

- **Grow your own.** Even a small garden can yield a significant harvest and save a lot of money on produce, especially if you freeze or preserve it for later. If your thumb is brown (like mine!), stick to easy-to-grow vegetables such as carrots, zucchini, cucumber, radishes, and squash. A simple herb garden with a few basics such as basil, cilantro, and parsley is also a great option!

- **Go frozen.** Frozen vegetables contain just as many nutrients as fresh ones but are usually much cheaper, which makes them a great alternative, especially in the months when there aren't many seasonal vegetables to choose from. They are a great option for most recipes, and while coupons for fresh produce are rare, there are plenty of frozen food coupons available that can be matched with store sales for a great deal!

Change the Way You Plan Meals

While stocking up on foods when they are at rock-bottom prices is the key component of cutting your grocery bill in half, all that food in your pantry won't do you much good if you aren't also able to adjust the way you plan your meals. Saving money on groceries and savvy meal planning go hand in hand.

Do you know your current meal planning and grocery shopping style? Who are you most like?

- **Gina Gourmet,** who loves to cook and spends a lot of time each week picking out elaborate, multi-ingredient recipes based solely on what she's in the mood for and not on what is in season or on sale. She considers herself a "foodie," and her grocery cart and refrigerator are full of organic, fresh vegetables and the best cuts of meat. She often finds herself throwing food away at the end of the week because she has purchased too much.

- **Lucy Last Minute,** who considers herself lucky just to get dinner on the table at all. Life is so hectic and busy that her "meal planning" happens on the fly—in the grocery store, when she is running through the aisles trying to remember what her family needs. She is in too much of a hurry to even bother to notice the prices, and since she's usually starving while shopping, she often ends up making a lot of impulse buys.

- **Ursula Unorganized,** who finds herself heading to the grocery store almost every single day because she is constantly forgetting something. She takes her meal planning one day at a time, because trying to plan a whole week at a time just seems far too overwhelming. Even when she does remember to make a list, half the time she ends up leaving it on the counter.

- **Brenda Boring,** whose family doesn't like to try new things, and so she buys pretty much the same foods every week, regardless of whether or not they are on sale. Her meal plan rarely varies, and her routine is so set in stone that most of the time she doesn't even bother making a list.

- **Sally Saver,** who plans her family's meals based solely on what's cheapest, even if it means cooking a meal or two that no one really likes. She hates spending a penny more than she has to and almost always opts for the generic store brand in order to save a little more. She thinks coupons are a waste of time because most of them are for expensive name-brand products that she would never buy anyway.

While these descriptions might not be entirely accurate, chances are you can identify with at least one of them! Most of us have a particular style we stick to, and adjusting old habits is by far the hardest part of learning to save on groceries.

Even so, no matter which style you currently identify with, your goal should be to become more like **Clever Carla**, who plans her meals based on what is already in her stockpile, and then on what is on sale at the grocery store. At the grocery store she pays attention to not just what she needs this week but which items are at their rock-bottom prices so she can add them to her stockpile. She also takes the time to find coupons that correspond with those rock-bottom prices in order to save even more.

If you normally wing it, like Lucy Last Minute or Ursula Unorganized, and find yourself running to the store several times a week, this step might not be as painful as you think. Instead of running to the store for dinner supplies, you'll be able to go to your stockpile — a ready-made grocery store right in your own pantry. You may even find that maintaining a varied stockpile by shopping the sales once a week saves you a lot of time, in addition to saving you from the expensive impulse and last-minute buys.

If you are a Brenda Boring, this will probably be a fairly easy adjustment to make as well. The biggest change will simply be learning to buy your family's favorites in larger quantities during the weeks they are on sale.

For all you Gina Gourmets who are accustomed to deciding what you want to eat and then writing your shopping list based on that plan, this adjustment may be a little harder. You will need to swap the order in which you do things, first determining what's on sale and what ingredients you already have on hand, and then making your meal plan accordingly, minimizing the number of nonsale items you need to buy each week. The good news is that of all the different meal planning styles, you are the one who will see the most dramatic drop in your grocery bill when you make this change!

All of you Sally Savers are actually doing pretty well, and of all the different styles, you are the ones who probably won't have to change much about the way you shop. That said, you may want to reconsider the idea of using coupons in correspondence with store sales. A few tweaks to your routine may even allow you enough leeway to stick to the foods your family truly enjoys.

If coming up with your own meal plan each week based on the store sales feels too overwhelming, you may want to check out an online meal planning service such as eMeals .com. This paid service offers a variety of different weekly,  budget-friendly meal plans, but my favorites are the ones that allow you to choose a specific store and then offer meal plans based on what's on sale at your grocery store that week. A corresponding app allows you to access the shopping list, menu, and recipes right on your phone or tablet. You can get an exclusive discount code by visiting www.livingwellspendingless.com/emeals or scanning the QR code on this page.

Use Coupons

It is not by accident that using coupons is discussed in the last section of this chapter and not the first. Coupons can and do help save a ton of money on your grocery bill, but *only if you follow these other steps first.* When and if you make these changes in the way you shop—getting into the habit of buying only what's on sale, buying enough to last your family six to eight weeks, saving on meat and produce, and adjusting the way you plan your meals to become more like Clever Carla—you will almost certainly notice a dramatic drop in your grocery bill, *even without clipping a single coupon.*

When you begin to match coupons to the things that are already on sale, you will see savings that are even more dramatic—50 to 60 percent off your normal grocery bill or even more! Doing this consistently, week after week, means you can literally cut your grocery bill in half.

Although shows like TLC's *Extreme Couponing* make it look a little scary, learning to match coupons to store sales is not nearly as confusing or intimidating as it may sound. Hundreds of websites are dedicated to helping people match coupons to store sales, and on my own website you can access an easy-to-follow series called *The Beginner's Guide to Coupons* that breaks down the whole process into manageable baby steps, explaining everything from where to find coupons to how to make your first shopping list to how to create a stockpile. You can get access to this for free at www.livingwellspendingless.com/BGTCoupons or by scanning the QR code on this page.

The important thing to remember is that coupons come last, not first. Don't buy something just because you have a coupon for it—the manufacturers count on you to do that! Wait for the sale and *then* use the coupon. There will always be more coupons than you can possibly use, and it is okay to let a coupon expire if that particular item never goes on sale. There will always be more coupons. Your patience will pay off in the long run! Furthermore, if using coupons seems too overwhelming or confusing, *don't worry about them!* Remember the secret I told you at the beginning of this chapter? The bulk of your savings will come from shopping the sales, stockpiling, and meal planning—*not* from coupons!

Finally, even if you are trying to avoid processed foods, don't automatically rule out the idea of using coupons. Coupons do exist for healthy options, including cheese, yogurt, and frozen vegetables, as well as for nonfood items we all need, such as toilet paper, shampoo, toothpaste, feminine hygiene products, cleaning products, and more.

Changing old patterns is never easy, but by making a few simple tweaks to the way you shop for groceries and plan your meals, you really can live well—and eat well—while spending less.

CHALLENGE: **Save on Food**

Commit to reducing your grocery bill as much as possible by adjusting the way you shop, stockpile, and plan meals. To establish a reasonable baseline for your grocery budget, go to www.cnpp.usda.gov/USDAFoodCost-Home.htm to see which category your current spending falls under—thrifty, low cost, moderate, or liberal. Depending on your current habits, shopping wisely may save you 10 percent or as much as 50 percent or more on your grocery bills.

Start your own rock-bottom price list to keep track of the best prices at your store, and work on buying items in bulk when they are at their very lowest price. You can find this list at www.living wellspendingless.com/pricelist/ or by scanning the QR code on this page.

Create a stockpile in your pantry or cupboards of the grocery staples and food items your family eats. Do not buy food just because it is on sale, but work on stockpiling the items you will actually use.

Adjust the way you plan your family's meals to use first what is in your stockpile and then what is on sale at the grocery store. Consider going meatless one or two days a week, and look for additional ways to save on meat and produce.

If you are already doing all of the above, consider learning how to save even more by using coupons. Access the free *Beginner's Guide to Coupons* at www.livingwellspendingless.com/BGTCoupons or scan the QR code on this page.

A Clean House Is a Happy House

Happiness does not consist in pastimes and amusements but in virtuous activities.

Aristotle

The wise woman builds her house,
   but with her own hands the foolish one tears
   hers down.

Proverbs 14:1

I am thankful for a lawn that needs mowing, windows that need cleaning, and gutters that need fixing because it means I have a home … I am thankful for the piles of laundry and ironing because it means my loved ones are nearby.

Nancie J. Carmody

*I*t was exactly the way Christmas vacation should be — relaxing, cozy, and completely laid-back. We stayed in our pajamas all day long, watching movies and building a whole city out of Legos on the floor. We ate leftover pie for breakfast and nibbled on the remains of our big dinner and all the holiday goodies dropped off by neighbors and friends. We left the dishes piled in the sink and let the garbage overflow while we played dominos and Candyland and took yet another nap.

It was great. At least for a few days.

But suddenly I'm not feeling quite so relaxed. Our Lego city has crumbled into a trail of tiny pieces scattered across the dog-hair-and-pine-needle-covered floor, and they are now painfully sharp blocks I have stepped on just one too many times. The kitchen table is so full of dominos and puzzle pieces that there is no place left to eat, which doesn't matter all that much because there isn't actually a single clean dish left in the house anyway. The beds haven't been made in days; the windows are covered in fingerprints; and there is a fine layer of dust covering every shelf and dresser. Everywhere I look, I see books and toys and clothes and clutter. My heart begins to race, and suddenly I feel like I might lose my mind if I have to sit in this mess for one more minute. *I just can't take it anymore!*

I gather my family into the living room. *Guess what,*

guys? I announce. *It's Operation Cleanup time!* The girls groan as I assign them their first task—picking each and every last Lego piece off the floor, while my husband starts by tackling the mountain of dirty dishes in what used to be our kitchen. I go into cleanup overdrive—making beds, collecting laundry, scrubbing the bathrooms, and clearing the clutter in one frenzied whirlwind of activity. Four hours later, every surface is sparkling. I take a deep breath. *That's better.*

Why I Make My Bed

A few years ago, I posted on my blog a list of simple rules that I wanted my family to live by. It included things like "pray daily," "eat your vegetables," "clean up after yourself," "use your manners," and "say sorry when you hurt someone." Funnily enough, the one rule people commented on more than any other was a line I honestly hadn't thought twice about including: "make your bed every day."

Is this really such a novel concept? I have to admit I tend to be slightly obsessive about making the bed each morning. I have even been guilty of making the bed while my husband is using the bathroom in the morning, even when I know he intends to go back to sleep! Until I posted my list of rules and saw how many people don't consider making the bed an essential part of their day, it had never even occurred to me this habit might be considered odd. But then, when I started to think about it, I realized there are some serious reasons why I take the time not just to make my bed but to clean and tidy my home each day as well:

- **It just looks better.** This reason should be fairly obvious, right? Straightened sheets and comforters with pillows in their proper place are far more aesthetically pleasing than disheveled blankets and a pile of pillows on the floor. A sink full of dirty dishes just looks ugly, whereas I could stare at my shiny appliances and sparkling-clean kitchen counters all day long. Windows and mirrors free of fingerprints are nicer to look at, while a freshly swept or vacuumed floor seems to instantly brighten the whole room. Likewise, toys, clothes, books, and all the other clutter that gets used on a daily basis look so much better when they are put away in their proper place rather than scattered all over the house.

- **I get more done when my house is clean.** Taking the time each day to focus on putting things in order always seems to jump-start my productivity, especially on those days I am in a hurry. I have noticed that when I ignore the mess and try to work around it, I am more easily distracted by whatever comes my way. On those days I'll often find I have accomplished almost nothing. It doesn't mean my house is always clean, but I do get more done on the days when it is.

- **I'm not embarrassed to have people over.** Both my husband and I love entertaining and throwing parties, and we greatly value hospitality. We want to be the kind of people who invite friends over to dinner on a moment's notice or can host an impromptu gathering without feeling stressed. When our house is clean, we are far more likely to invite people over on the spur of the moment, and I don't mind if people show up unannounced. It may sound silly, but one of my proudest moments as a stay-at-home mom was the day my husband and four of his coworkers popped by totally unexpectedly in the middle of the day after attending a meeting nearby. The house was spotless; the girls were napping; and I was working on a project at the kitchen table. My husband later told me they were shocked at how calm and inviting our home felt, and how they couldn't believe I had no idea they would be coming by.

- **I can find things.** It is so much easier to find what I am looking for when everything is put away in its proper place. And, just as importantly, it is so much easier to put things away when everything actually has a proper place.

- **My kids play (and learn) better.** Even with the vast majority of their toys taken away, my darling girls still seem to have an amazing ability to make a mess almost instantaneously. Do your kids possess this talent? Sometimes it seems they spend their entire day just dragging out all the books, games, and Legos they can find, just so they can leave them on the floor. Even so, I've noticed that when we keep their room clean (and they are very involved in this process), they actually play much better. Just like me, they can find the thing they are looking for and can focus on just one thing at a time instead of being overwhelmed by everything they own staring at them from the floor.

- **It makes my family happy.** No one wants to live in

chaos, and no one wants to come home after a hard day at work or school to a home that is a disaster zone. Don't get me wrong. In my family there are plenty of days when we let our mess get out of control and suddenly the kids are hungry, crabby, and screaming; dishes are piled in the sink; dinner isn't prepared; the rest of the house is in disarray; and the laundry is piled sky-high. But on the days when the house is clean and things are in order, we all seem to get along a little better. We linger at the dinner table just a little longer and enjoy life just a little more.

- **I am more creative.** Instead of seeing nothing but the mess, my mind is clear to see the creative potential around me, and my desk and table are clear to spread out and complete a project. When it comes to writing, I have a much easier time with the entire process if my office is neat and tidy when I begin. Likewise, when my kitchen is clean and organized, I'm a lot more motivated to get creative with my cooking and baking. I know a little mess doesn't bother some people, but I have a really hard time creating anything — or enjoying those creative moments — when I am surrounded by dirt and clutter.

- **It helps me get a good night's sleep.** There is nothing I love more than crawling into a carefully made bed. It is so comforting! Rather than needing to wrestle with tangled sheets or scoop up dusty blankets from the floor, I am instantly relaxed and ready for a night of rejuvenation. Even if I can't manage to do much to clean or tidy the rest of the house, I almost always do this one task because I can't stand sleeping in a messy bed. A made bed feels better; the blankets stay on all night long; and I sleep much better.

- **It's my job.** For me, to be grown-up means I accept responsibility for taking care of my home. When my husband and I first got married, we both agreed we always wanted to have at least one of us at home with our kids, and that the one who stayed home would be responsible for running the household and keeping house. Colossians 3:23 tells us, "Whatever you do, work at it with all your heart, as working for the Lord, not for human masters." If my job is to take care of the home, my duty is to do it well. This is not to say that the other one shouldn't help out or that we don't sometimes share duties; we do. That said, we also accept the fact that keeping house is just part of having a home, as well as a way to show each other we care.

I haven't always been such a neat freak. Growing up, I was the kid who couldn't keep my room clean and who, when told to clean up, would shove everything under the bed or in the closet and hope no one noticed. In college, the house I shared with three roommates was barely habitable, to say the least. The only time one of us would clean a dish was when there were no clean ones left. Our hideously ugly, low-rent 1970s duplex with its broken paneling, threadbare carpet, and mismatched garage-sale furniture didn't exactly inspire any of us to keep things neat and tidy.

Things changed when I finished college and got a real job and, for the first time, my very own apartment. I painted the walls, hung pictures, and raided the local IKEA for cute but inexpensive furniture that actually matched. I finally had a home of my own that I wanted to take care of, and I started to realize how satisfying it felt to come home every day to a space I loved.

I am no longer a single girl in a tiny apartment. Having a bigger house and a husband and kids to contribute to the mess, along with a thousand obligations pulling me in all different directions, means there are plenty of days when my house is a complete disaster. In fact, sometimes by the end of the day it's a disaster—even though I have spent time cleaning up. But that's life. Keeping a house clean is a thankless, never-ending job, whether you work full-time or stay home all day, whether you have one child or ten children. While I try to give myself grace on those days when I can't pull it all together, I still think it is important to put in the effort. When all is said and done, if my house is clean and my bed is made, I breathe a little easier.

A Cleaning Routine That Works

Of course, knowing all the reasons for keeping your house clean isn't worth a whole lot if you can't find a practical cleaning routine that works for your own life and your own family. While there is no one "right" method that will work for everyone, the essential first step to any effective cleaning schedule is simply deciding to make a clean house a priority. Your house will never magically clean itself; you have to work at it. Accepting the responsibility and putting in the time to make it happen are ultimately the only ways to get the job done.

Over the years I have seen and tried lots of cleaning routines. Some people prefer to clean all at once, either once a week or waiting until things get so dirty they can't take it anymore—and then spend a whole day, or at least several hours, scrubbing toilets, dusting surfaces, mopping floors, and catching up on laundry. Others prefer to tackle one major task per day, cleaning the bathrooms on Monday, vacuuming on Tuesday, doing the laundry on Wednesday, and so on.

I have personally found a daily speed cleaning routine to be the most effective way to keep my house clean, even though now these duties are shared with my husband. Between the two of us, we probably spend, on average, about an hour each day making our home sparkle, which ends up being at least seven hours a week in cleaning time. This is a significant amount of time! That said, for the reasons I shared earlier, we both believe it is well worth spending seven hours a week cleaning in order to have a house that is neat and tidy most of the time. The trick, we have discovered, is staying on top of it.

I am a list kind of girl, so I like to have a daily cleaning checklist. Of course, getting my husband to use it is another story! You can print my speed cleaning checklist at www.livingwellspending less.com/speedcleaning or scan the QR code on this page. In our house, the checklist is located on our "control center" wall, where we have a dry-erase

monthly calendar and also a spot for a weekly meal plan and important phone numbers. Since it is all in one place, we can easily check the calendar for pressing activities or appointments. This helps us prioritize our cleaning activities and cut things out or add extra tasks as necessary.

We don't use a wide variety of cleaning supplies, and we aren't picky about brands. In fact, although we used to use a lot of commercial products, including convenient (but expensive), disposable antibacterial cleaning wipes, we have slowly transitioned to using a small selection of homemade cleaning products. Not only are they cheaper, but they smell better, contain fewer allergens, are better for the environment, and require us to keep far fewer bottles of stuff lying around. The "recipes" for our favorite cleaners are found later in this chapter.

Here is my speed cleaning routine:

GENERAL GUIDELINES

- Start at one end of the house and work your way to the other end.

- Cleaning is much easier when everything has a home. Work on creating organized storage for all the clutter that ends up getting scattered around the house, like school papers, mail, shoes, and toys.

- Use a large laundry basket to collect items such as toys or clothing that need to be returned to a different room. After you have finished cleaning every room, take a few moments to put away the collected items.

- Save sweeping, mopping, and vacuuming until the end

and then do it all at once. If you have mostly hard-surface floors, use an industrial dry mop to wipe the floors each day, then wet mop once or twice a week. Vacuuming once or twice a week is usually plenty for most homes.

- Save glass cleaning for the end as well, spot-checking doors, windows, and mirrors, as well as bathroom fixtures and sinks.
- Keep daily shower cleaner in the shower area, and spray down after each use.
- Store your toilet brush in a container of bleach; replace the bleach once a week.

BEDROOMS (5 to 10 minutes each)

- Make the bed.
- Pick up any clothes, toys, or dishes lying around.
- Use a duster or dry rag to dust all surfaces, including the headboard and footboard.

BATHROOMS (5 to 10 minutes each)

- Clear counters and pick up any items from the floor.
- Squirt toilet bowl cleaner or all-purpose cleaner around rim; let sit.
- Wipe down sinks, shower, and bathtub with a wet rag and disinfectant spray or wipes.
- Use toilet brush to scrub toilet bowl and rim.
- Wipe down toilet seat and lid with disinfectant spray or wipes; also wipe down surrounding floor.

LIVING AREAS (10 to 15 minutes)

- Pick up any shoes, dishes, toys, books, or other items lying around.
- Use a duster or rag to dust all surfaces.
- Use a damp cloth to wipe down leather furniture, tables, and dining chairs.
- Tidy desk area and make sure all paperwork and mail is sorted and filed.

KITCHEN (10 to 15 minutes)

- Fill sink with hot soapy water.
- Pick up any items that don't belong in kitchen; clear counters of all food and dirty dishes.
- Unload and reload dishwasher.
- Hand-wash dishes and pots or pans as needed.
- Spray all counters with disinfectant spray and then use soapy water and a wet sponge to wipe them down.
- Wipe down stovetop.
- Dry and put away any hand-washed dishes; then drain and rinse sink.

FINISHING UP

- Use a dry mop to clean hard floors. Spot clean with a sponge if necessary. Use a wet mop once a week.
- Vacuum rugs and carpets once or twice a week.
- Clean glass surfaces and mirrors as needed with glass

cleaner and a lint-free rag. Don't forget to spray and wipe the bathroom fixtures for extra shine.

- Put away all items collected in laundry basket while cleaning.

While a speed cleaning routine is my own preference, it may not work for everyone. For more tips and printable worksheets to help you create a cleaning schedule that works for you in just three easy steps, visit www.livingwellspendingless .com/cleaningschedule or scan the QR code on this page.

It may take a little getting used to, but developing a cleaning system that works is ultimately the best way to enjoy your home to its fullest. And don't forget to enlist your children's help with these chores. They are part of your team, and they'll need to have these skills when they're on their own. A clean home is a happy home!

Green and Thrifty
Homemade Cleaners

Throughout much of my adult life, I've had a bad habit of thinking that more cleaning supplies would result in a cleaner house. At one point we had so many mops and brooms in our broom closet that my husband finally exploded in exasperation: "You do realize that none of them actually clean the floor for you, right?" Of course, until he pointed it out, I think I actually thought they might.

A key component of a clean house is to *stop* bringing in more things, so before you run out to buy all the ingredients for making your own cleaners, be sure to *first use up* all those cleaning supplies you already have sitting in your cabinet. Using what you already have is about as thrifty as you can get!

For any cleaning supplies you do still need, you may be surprised to discover you probably have most of the ingredients right in your own kitchen or laundry cabinet. I have been amazed to discover that a combination of just a few common household products can tackle almost every cleaning task. In fact, I've discovered that  just ten different products, most of which I already keep on hand, can be combined in ten different ways to make ten awesome, green, and super-thrifty cleaning products. The ingredients and recipes are listed below, but you can also get a handy printable sheet with all ten recipes at www.livingwellspendingless.com/greencleaning or scan the QR code on this page.

The Ingredients

1. White vinegar
2. Baking soda
3. Lemons or lemon juice
4. Salt
5. Olive oil
6. Ivory bar soap

7. Liquid dishwashing soap
8. Arm & Hammer Super Washing Soda
9. Borax
10. Assorted essential oils (I like lemon, lemongrass, and eucalyptus)

The Cleaning Recipes

1. BATHROOM CLEANER

3/4 cup baking soda
1/4 cup lemon juice (about half a lemon)
3 tablespoons salt
3 tablespoons liquid dishwashing soap
1/2 cup vinegar
10 drops essential oil (optional)

Mix all ingredients together in a medium bowl to make a paste; use scrub brush or sponge to apply to tub, shower walls, and sinks. Be sure to test a small area to make sure paste does not scuff tub surface; if it does, eliminate the salt from the mixture! Rinse well with warm water and a wet rag; then dry with an old towel. Discard excess.

2. TOILET BOWL SUPER CLEANER

1 cup baking soda
1 cup vinegar
10 drops essential oil (optional)

Turn off flow valve to toilet and flush once or twice until water is drained. Pour in baking soda; then slowly pour in vinegar, being sure to get the vinegar to cover as much of the bowl surface as possible. Add a few drops of essential oil. The baking soda will react with the vinegar. After the reaction is done, use a toilet brush to scrub the surface and remove any rings or stains. Turn water back on and flush.

3. FURNITURE POLISH

3/4 cup olive oil
2 tablespoons lemon juice (about a quarter of a lemon)
1 tablespoon vinegar
3–4 drops lemon essential oil (optional)

Blend ingredients together in small bowl. To use, dampen rag in warm water and squeeze out excess. Dip damp rag into furniture polish; then wipe on surface of furniture. Buff off with an old, dry towel. Can also be used to polish stainless steel. Store in an airtight container up to six weeks.

4. GLASS CLEANER

1 1/2 cups vinegar
1 1/2 cups water
5 to 10 drops essential oil (optional)

Mix vinegar, water, and essential oil in spray bottle. Spray on glass and use squeegee, crumpled newspaper (use newspaper that is at least two weeks old to avoid black fingers), or a lint-free rag to get a streak-free shine. This solution also works well for shining chrome and countertops after they have been disinfected. Keeps indefinitely.

5. ALL-PURPOSE CLEANING SPRAY

1 tablespoon Borax
1 tablespoon Arm & Hammer Super Washing Soda
1 teaspoon liquid dishwashing soap
1 cup vinegar
4 cups hot water
25 to 30 drops essential oil (optional)

Whisk all ingredients well in a large bowl; then pour into spray bottle. Spray on and wipe surface clean with a damp cloth. Can be used to clean and disinfect almost any surface.

6. STAINLESS STEEL CLEANER

2 tablespoons baking soda
1/2 cup vinegar
2 cups warm water

Mix ingredients in spray bottle. Mixture will foam up; when it stops bubbling, put on cap and spray stainless steel surface; then wipe clean and dry with a lint-free rag. To add extra shine, use furniture polish instructions above.

7. DISHWASHER DETERGENT

1 cup baking soda
1 cup Borax
1/2 cup salt
1 to 2 drops liquid dish soap (optional)
vinegar

Mix first three ingredients well and store in an airtight container. To use, add one tablespoon of the mixture to each compartment in your dishwasher, and add two tablespoons of vinegar to your rinse compartment. If you have any problems with clumping, you may want to add one drop of liquid dish soap to the soap container before putting in the powder. Also, if you have hard water and are noticing spots on your dishes, you may want to consider adding Lemi Shine or citric acid to your mixture.

8. FLOOR CLEANER

1 cup vinegar
1/2 cup baking soda
8 to 10 cups hot water
1 tablespoon Borax
1 tablespoon Arm & Hammer Super Washing Soda
20 to 30 drops essential oil (optional)

Mix together vinegar and baking soda in bucket; add hot water, Borax, washing soda, and essential oil. Mix until all powder is dissolved. Use mop or sponge to wipe down floor with mixture; wipe dry with clean towel. Discard excess.

9. LAUNDRY DETERGENT

1 bar Ivory soap
1 cup Borax
1 cup Arm & Hammer Super Washing Soda

Place Ivory soap in a large microwave-safe bowl.

Heat in the microwave for two minutes, until soap turns to foam. Quickly stir fvoam until it becomes small soap chips. (If soap chips are too large, pulse in food processor.) Mix well with Borax and washing soda. Allow to cool completely; then store in airtight container. Use 1 to 2 tablespoons of mixture per load. Please note that this detergent works best in warm or hot water; for cold water, or if you are using a front-load washer, first dissolve powder in 1/4 cup of hot water before using.

---

10. FABRIC SOFTENER

1/4 to 1/2 cup vinegar
essential oil (optional)

Add vinegar with several drops of your favorite essential oil to the rinse cycle or to the fabric softener compartment of your front-load washer.

No Place Like (a Clean) Home

While there are plenty of compelling reasons to keep a neat and tidy house, I think the best one of all is perhaps this: a clean house saves money. Taking good care of your house and possessions means that appliances, furniture, carpets, and other items within your home are far less likely to get damaged or broken. Furthermore, when you know your things will be taken care of, you are more willing to invest in high-quality pieces that will stand the test of time and save money over the long run rather than in cheap junk that doesn't last. Consistently putting things away where they belong also means your things are less likely to get lost, which again saves money because you won't be buying replacements.

Finally, a clean house makes it nice to simply be at home. Unlike almost every other place on earth, staying home is free. I don't know about you, but when my house is messy, all I want to do is escape the clutter. For me this has usually meant going to Target and mindlessly filling a cart with even more things we don't need, which ultimately just adds to the chaos. When my house is neat and tidy, it becomes my own little haven, an oasis from the hustle and bustle—and expense—of the outside world. When my house is clean, there is no place I'd rather be.

CHALLENGE: Clean Your House

Spend some time thinking about your own reasons for keeping a tidy house. Is this something you strive for? Why or why not? What for you are the most compelling reasons to clean? Do an honest assessment of your current housekeeping routine. Is your house usually fairly tidy, or is it often a mess? How much time do you spend doing housework each day? Is it enough? Too much? Too little?

If you don't currently have a cleaning routine that works, commit for the next four weeks to a daily speed cleaning routine like the one outlined in this chapter, or use the printable worksheets at livingwellspending less.com to customize a schedule that fits your own family's needs (visit www.livingwellspendingless .com/cleaningschedule or access the QR code on this page).

Finally, as you test out this new routine, pay close attention to any changes in your own psyche or in your family dynamics over the next few weeks. How does having a clean house change your environment? Are you able to get more done? Do you enjoy being home more? Do you feel happier? What *don't* you like about it?

The Best Things in Life Are Free

You aren't really wealthy until you
have something that money can't buy.

Garth Brooks

Set your hearts on things above,
where Christ is, seated at the right
hand of God. Set your minds on
things above, not on earthly things.

Colossians 3:1–2

He who loses money, loses much; he
who loses a friend, loses much more;
he who loses faith, loses all.

Eleanor Roosevelt

"We should be in heaven," I say, looking out toward the sparkling aqua-blue water gently crashing over the white sand beach. From the veranda of our four-bedroom guest "cottage," I look back toward the palatial main house, with its white stucco walls, two-story windows, and terra-cotta tiled roof, wondering exactly what we are supposed to do now. From the moment we arrived, things have been, well, just a little awkward.

"Aw, c'mon, it will be fun," Chuck said when the invitation to spend the weekend at Nadine and Andrew's beach house arrived. "We should go. Besides, how often do we get to hang out with millionaires and see how the other half lives? It's like our own real-life episode of *Lifestyles of the Rich and Famous!*"

I wasn't *quite* so enthusiastic. "I'm just not sure we have anything in common with them. I don't like feeling we have nothing to contribute. The last time we visited, it just felt weird not to be able to pay our own way. And besides, you don't see the things she posts on Facebook, asking for recommendations on hotels in Dubai and sharing pictures of their newest thoroughbred. It's a little hard to relate."

Chuck just laughed. "Don't you think you might be exaggerating just a little? I know they have a lot of money, but they are also really nice. Let's say yes. It is practically like being offered a free vacation."

But it doesn't *feel* like a vacation, even though it certainly looks like one. Our cottage truly couldn't be lovelier, and it is certainly fancier than any hotel we've ever stayed at. The glass-tiled shower has no less than fourteen showerheads, and the bathroom is stocked with toiletries from L'Occitane. The sheets on the carefully made king-sized bed are as soft as butter, and the gourmet kitchen puts my own recently remodeled kitchen to shame. The white sectional in the "beach casual" living room looks so pristine that I am almost afraid to sit on it, and turning on the eighty-inch flat screen proves to be so complicated that I eventually give up, though I do manage to turn on the fireplace inadvertently after pressing enough buttons.

No, the problem with this vacation is not the accommodations. Instead, something just seems off. Awkward. Perhaps we are just out of our league, but the only thing our kids really want to do is play on the beach. Instead, we are obligated to follow the agenda we have been given, which includes tennis lessons, horseback riding, and sailing, followed by dinner at the main house. It all sounds like fun on paper, but the reality is anything but. We're not sure what to do or say. Every conversation seems focused on things we know nothing about—horses and sailboats and last season's wine crop, how difficult it is to find good help these days, where Nadine and Andrew plan to travel to next, and how bored they've become with the status quo. They don't ask about our lives. I don't think it even crosses their minds. We smile and nod politely and try to relate because, well, what else can we do? We are the guests. We are supposed to be grateful, even if it feels a little like we are employees being paid to act like "friends."

And anyway, isn't this exactly the life I always dreamed of?

It suddenly occurs to me that Nadine and Andrew literally have *everything* they could possibly want in life, more than most people even dream of. Multiple homes in the best locations, designer wardrobes, gourmet food, dozens of fancy cars, and a staff to attend to their every need. They don't really have a care in the world, and yet they don't seem especially happy. Although I think they mean well, and despite inviting us to spend the weekend at their estate, they haven't actually shown a whole lot of hospitality, at least not in the sense of making us feel at home. The idea of spending the day just sitting on the beach creating a sand castle is completely foreign to them. It appears they are so accustomed to paying to get what they want that they've missed the beauty of the simple things—of true friendship and hospitality and creativity. Instead of creating joy, they try to purchase it.

Don't they know that almost all the best things in life are free?

Nurturing Your Friendships

At our very core, we all want to be loved and accepted. We crave those special friendships that will build us up and keep us going when times are tough. We long for someone to laugh with, someone to cry with, and someone to cheer us on. Even so, I think many of us struggle when it comes to making and maintaining true friendships. Life gets hectic, and it is hard to keep tabs on your own life, much less someone else's. We forgo real relationships for the superficial Facebook variety, convincing ourselves that if we just Like enough status updates, we will be caught up with our friends' lives.

But over the years I have learned the most important lesson of friendship is also the most basic: *In order to have a friend, you must be a friend.* Some of the loneliest people I know are those who sit around waiting for other people to reach out and then wonder why they don't have any friends. They feel ignored, unappreciated, or unwanted, and grow resentful when they see other people cultivating friendships that seem to come naturally, and yet it never occurs to them to make the first move, to reach out with a smile or a kind word. When was the last time you reached out to a friend to find out how *they* were doing, without the ulterior motive of sharing your own latest news? When was the last time you picked up the phone just to catch up, or dropped off a meal just because you knew they could probably use it? When was the last time you invited a friend out for lunch, or even sent a text message to see what was new?

It takes effort and intentionality to be a good friend. It means being willing to put yourself out there and risk rejection, but the rewards of true friendship are always worth the risk. Here are a few practical ideas to help renew old connections and build strong friendships:

- **Make a list.** Write down the names of all your friends or acquaintances with whom you'd like to more intentionally pursue a closer friendship. It could include old friends you may have lost touch with or newer friends you'd like to get to know better. Keep the list close at hand and begin thinking of ways to connect with those who are on it.

- **Pray.** It is almost impossible not to care deeply for the people you are praying for. Begin praying daily for those friends on your list. If you're not sure what to pray for, consider sending a text or email or picking up the phone to ask for specific prayer requests. A couple of years ago, a friend of mine sent me a text message, out of the blue, asking how she could pray for me that week. I was so touched that I decided to follow suit. Although I do sometimes forget, each Monday morning I try to send a quick text to a handful of my close friends so I can then spend a few minutes each day praying for their specific needs. It takes so little of my time, and yet it has been such an integral part of building, transforming, and even healing those relationships.

- **Block out time.** If friendships are to be a priority in your life, you have to be purposeful about making time for your friends, even when you are busy. *Especially when you are busy.* This might mean setting a regular coffee or lunch date or planning a monthly girls' night out or a game night for couples. You could try taking turns hosting each other's family or making a plan to connect for donuts after church. The point is not what you do but that you make the effort. Your friendships will grow and flourish only if you are willing to put in the time.

- **Reach out.** Don't wait for others to reach out to you,

and don't waste your time on bitterness because you feel ignored or forgotten. Chances are you haven't been ignored or forgotten; rather, the friend you think no longer remembers you is feeling just as busy or overwhelmed or neglected as you are. Be willing to make the first move toward building a better friendship, and chances are those friends you reach out to will reciprocate in turn. Likewise, pay attention to others who seem lonely or lost — the neighbor who just moved in next door, the new family at church, the shy mom at Bible study who never says a word — and be the first to offer a kind word or compliment, or to ask them about themselves. You'll be amazed at how far a little interest in others will go!

- **Show grace.** Our friends will inevitably disappoint us. They will hurt our feelings. They will annoy us. They will forget to show up or say something stupid or make a decision we don't agree with. They will be flawed and imperfect and inadequate. In other words, they will be human. To have a friend, we must be a friend, and ultimately, that means showing grace when our friends don't come through the way we want them to. It means forgiving when necessary, looking for the good instead of the bad, treating them the way we'd like to be treated.

The truth is that we all tend to get wrapped up in our own little worlds and forget to nurture our friendships like we should. Even so, taking the time to reach out without expecting anything in return and to cultivate close friendships are some of the most rewarding and meaningful activities we will ever do. Don't miss the opportunity to be a great friend!

True friendship is free.

Practicing Hospitality

Friendship and hospitality go hand in hand. Too often we make the mistake of thinking that hospitality is all about showing off our beautiful homes or Pinterest-perfect party preparations or fancy cooking skills. We become so concerned with impressing our guests with our designer décor, spotless bathrooms, and gourmet food that we forget all about making them feel welcome. Or because our home doesn't look exactly the way we want it to or because we can't afford a gourmet menu, we assume we're just not meant to entertain. We don't realize hospitality has almost nothing to do with what our house looks like or what food we serve. As my friend Edie puts it, "Hospitality is not about inviting people into our perfect homes; it is all about inviting people into our imperfect hearts."

What our guests really want, at their core, is not a five-star hotel or an elaborate spread, but to feel at home — to feel they are wanted and that they belong. All the money in the world can't buy that kind of hospitality, because it comes from the heart and not the store. True hospitality is sitting down with our guests to ask about *their* day and about *their* lives, looking them in the eye and letting them know, from our words and actions, that *we are glad they are there*. It is making them feel like having them in our home is not an inconvenience or a burden, but a joy. It is giving them our full attention and attending to *their* needs. True hospitality is not about us, but about *the guest*.

Over and over, the Bible testifies to the importance of showing love to others through hospitality:

"'For I was hungry and you gave me something to eat, I was thirsty and you gave me something to drink, I was a stranger and you invited me in, I needed clothes and you clothed me, I was sick and you looked after me, I was in prison and you came to visit me.'

"Then the righteous will answer him, 'Lord, when did we see you hungry and feed you, or thirsty and give you something to drink? When did we see you a stranger and invite you in, or needing clothes and clothe you? When did we see you sick or in prison and go to visit you?'

"The King will reply, 'Truly I tell you, whatever you did for one of the least of these brothers and sisters of mine, you did for me.'"

MATTHEW 25:35–40

Share with the Lord's people who are in need. Practice hospitality.

ROMANS 12:13

Do not forget to show hospitality to strangers, for by so doing some people have shown hospitality to angels without knowing it.

HEBREWS 13:2

Above all, love each other deeply, because love covers

over a multitude of sins. Offer hospitality to one another without grumbling.

1 PETER 4:8–9

If showing hospitality still feels overwhelming, here are a few tips that may help you put your guests at ease:

- **Anticipate their needs.** Sometimes achieving this is as simple as putting yourself in your guests' shoes. Will they be hungry or thirsty when they arrive? Tired after a long drive or flight? Will they need to cool off on a hot day or warm up after coming in from the chill? Will they need to use the restroom? Do they have any health concerns you will need to accommodate? Do they have trouble going up and down stairs, or will you need to make arrangements or childproof the house to prepare for little kids? Making the effort to think about how your guests might feel when they arrive, and then actively working to make things as comfortable as possible, can make all the difference.

- **Plan ahead.** The best way to avoid making your guests feel like a burden is to avoid rushing around in front of them. Show your guests you care and that you are happy they are there by not leaving preparations until the last minute. If you are cooking dinner, do as much ahead of time as possible so when your guests arrive, you can give them your full attention. If you are hosting overnight guests, figure out where everyone will sleep and make up the beds ahead of time.

- **Make conversation.** The quickest, most surefire way to get someone talking and a conversation rolling is to ask your guest or guests a few questions about themselves. Be interested in what they have to say, and listen to the answers. More often than not, taking the time to show genuine interest in someone else's life or thoughts is all it takes to make them feel at ease. If you are hosting a large gathering with multiple guests, take the time to not only introduce those who are new but to make sure the conversation gets going. Have you ever shown up at a party where you didn't know anyone and not a single person talked to you? Don't do that to your guests! Instead, make the effort to introduce strangers by letting them know what they might have in common.

- **Smile.** A simple smile can go a long way in making people feel at ease. If you look stressed or bored or annoyed, your guests will pick up on it and will feel like they are an intrusion rather than a blessing.

- **Avoid awkward moments.** Once again, making your guests feel comfortable means putting yourself in their shoes and anticipating their needs. We once visited some friends on their farm, expecting to go horseback riding and fishing, only to arrive and find out they had planned an outing to a fancy restaurant that we were completely unprepared and underdressed for. In preparing for mealtimes, try to ask about dietary restrictions or allergies ahead of time to avoid any unexpected issues. Finally, whatever you do, don't ask your guests to pick sides in a disagreement between you and your spouse!

When we let go of the idea that hospitality is all about

impressing others with *what we have,* we suddenly realize the opportunities to show them *who we are* are all around us. Don't wait until you think you're ready, because you might never be. Instead, invite others—friends, family, and even strangers—into your imperfect heart as often as you can. You won't regret it.

True hospitality is free.

Cultivating Creativity

Sometimes we don't realize how creative we really are until we are forced to be. Going to the store is easy. Buying what we want is easy. It requires no imagination, no innovation, no original thought whatsoever. We buy what we see in front of us, just because it is there. But the funny thing about creativity is that it is usually born out of limitations rather than out of abundance. The less we have, the more creative we must be. Sometimes cultivating our own creativity is as simple as learning to embrace our boundaries and restraints.

It is important to note that craftiness is not the same as creativity. I have always thought of myself as a "crafty" person. I love sewing and crafting and all things DIY, and I never met a Mod Podge project I didn't love, but none of those things necessarily make me "creative." I can go online and simply copy all the great projects I see on Pinterest or other websites and never truly create something of my own. My husband, on the other hand, is certainly *not* crafty at all. He is an engineer through and through—methodical, thorough, and a total perfectionist. But he is extremely creative when it comes to solving problems. He will methodically examine an issue from all angles and often come up with ideas I would have never thought of in a million years. I have other friends who are completely hopeless with a glue gun or sewing machine, but who display nothing less than creative genius in the kitchen or who can write the most beautiful, heartfelt thank-you notes without giving it a second thought. Ultimately I think we all have the capacity for creativity in our own way.

Ephesians 2:10 tells us, "For we are God's handiwork, created in Christ Jesus to do good works, which God prepared in advance for us to do." God doesn't make mistakes, and we are all created in his image to do his work. We all have the capacity to creatively use the gifts he has given us so we may ultimately glorify him. Creativity is not a trip to the craft store; it is a willingness to think outside the box in order to use the resources *you already have* in new and innovative ways. It is also a willingness to try and sometimes fail. Not all of us will be good at everything, but sometimes you don't know until you try!

Here are some ways to cultivate more creativity in your own life:

- **Read more.** How much time do you spend reading each week? The more you read, the more you know; and unlike watching television, reading actually engages your brain and makes it work better. Read everything you can get your hands on, from newspaper columns to magazine articles to books, both fiction and nonfiction. Read to your kids too—children's books are always the best! Just keep reading.

- **Reflect.** Are you taking a step back every now and then? Give yourself the time and space to ponder the people, events, and goings-on of your daily life. Keep a journal where you are free to be introspective and to self-reflect your current circumstances.

- **Ask questions.** Do you want to know more about what is happening around you? Don't take the world at face value, but instead be willing to dig deeper. Take the time to ask why or how or when, or even why not.

- **Pay attention.** Are you truly tuned in? Take the time to really listen when people are talking to you and to actually see what is going on. Put away your phone or tablet and instead watch and listen and absorb the reality of your world.

- **Play.** When was the last time you really played with your kids? Don't be afraid to get down on the floor and lose yourself while playing with Legos or dolls or coloring a picture. Likewise, spend time outside and play hide-and-seek or tag or kick the can just for fun.

- **Brainstorm.** Are you ready to record your thoughts when inspiration strikes? If you tend to get your ideas at a certain time, say, when lying in bed or scrubbing the floors, make sure you have a way of remembering them close at hand. For instance, I find I often get the best ideas while I'm driving, so I will use my iPhone to dictate notes so I don't forget them.

- **Rest.** Are you getting enough sleep? Our brains need a chance to recharge and refresh, and the only way to do this is through sleep. I am often the worst offender when it comes to not getting enough rest, but I have found that more sleep means I have more energy to make it through the day, a stronger immune system to ward off illness, and ultimately more creativity because my brain is fully turned on.

- **Cultivate and enjoy the creativity of the people around you.** Celebrating the talent in other people is a great way to find inspiration in your own life. Allow yourself to enjoy the unique contributions your friends may add to your life without feeling jealous or envious that you don't possess the same skills. If there is something your friend is good at, consider asking them to teach you or share a little of their knowledge. Perhaps you could even reciprocate by sharing something of your own.

Inspiration is everywhere, although sometimes it is just a matter of opening our eyes to see the beauty right in front of us. It is all too easy to get weighed down with the busyness of life's obligations, by the stress of not having enough money, by the heartache of disappointment and tragedy, or by the loneliness of not having close friends. We are so easily fixated on the talents, gifts, and resources we *don't* have that it completely clouds our ability to see all those things we *do* have, which we can use to enrich our own lives and those around us.

Cultivating and embracing our own creativity, in whatever form it may take, ultimately only serve to make our lives better. Real joy and satisfaction comes from solving a problem or maximizing our resources or creating something beautiful out of our own two hands. And true creativity is free.

CHALLENGE: Embrace the Things That Matter Most

Take stock of your current friendships. Are they flourishing or floundering? Why or why not? How could you make them stronger? Write down the names of three friends or acquaintances you would like to reach out to over the next few weeks; then write down the specific ways in which you will reach out to each one. Will you call? Send a note? Invite them to lunch or coffee? Spend time praying for these friends as well, and begin making a conscious effort to nurture and develop those relationships.

Spend time reflecting on your own attitude toward hospitality. Do you enjoy hosting others in your home, or is this something you normally avoid? How can you make showing hospitality a greater priority in your life?

Finally, think about the role of creativity in your own life. How are you using the resources you've been given to enrich your own life and those around you? What could you do to cultivate more creativity in your life?

We Get More When We Give

Happiness does not result from what we get, but from what we give.

Ben Carson

What good is it, my brothers and sisters, if someone claims to have faith but has no deeds? Can such faith save them? Suppose a brother or sister is without clothes and daily food. If one of you says to them, "Go in peace; keep warm and well fed," but does nothing about their physical needs, what good is it? In the same way, faith by itself, if it is not accompanied by action, is dead.

James 2:14–17

We make a living by what we get. We make a life by what we give.

Winston Churchill

I *wish there was some way to get out of it,* I think to myself as the alarm goes off, and I contemplate hitting the snooze button one more time. I let out a heavy sigh, wondering *what on earth* I was thinking to commit to teaching Sunday school again this year. All I *really* want to do at this moment is stay in my cozy bed for the rest of the morning, maybe even the rest of the day. It is Sunday, after all. Isn't this supposed to be my day of rest? I work so hard all week long. Why should I have to give up my one day of relaxation just to teach a bunch of second and third graders a lesson they'll probably forget as soon as they get home. *Maybe I could call in sick.*

But I can't call in sick. I know there are people who are counting on me, and I don't want to let them down. Instead I reluctantly drag myself out of bed, pour a cup of coffee, and sit down to plan my lesson for the day.

This month we're talking about David. I've never really spent a lot of time reading about David, mostly because in my own devotions I usually prefer to stick to the seemingly more practical takeaways and easy-to-understand instructions found in the New Testament. I look up today's story about Samuel choosing and anointing David, which is found in 1 Samuel 16.

Samuel is told by God to go to Bethlehem to anoint one of the sons of Jesse as the new king. Jesse lines up his sons, and Samuel is instantly impressed by the oldest, who is tall and handsome. *Surely he must be the guy*, Samuel says to himself. But that wasn't the guy. Instead, God says to Samuel, "Do not consider his appearance or his height, for I have rejected him. The LORD does not look at the things people look at. People look at the outward appearance, but the LORD looks at the heart" (verse 7). As it turned out, David was so insignificant, so unimpressive, so completely un-kinglike, that *he wasn't even invited* to the party. He was the one stuck tending the sheep.

As I sit there, drinking my coffee and trying to wake up, I am completely taken by this story. This isn't exactly how I pictured the great and mighty King David. But the message is clear: God doesn't see what we see.

An hour later, I am sitting on a carpet square that does almost nothing to cushion the hard floor of my Sunday school room. Surrounded by brightly painted walls and ten boisterous seven- and eight-year-olds, I look at their eager faces, not totally sure how to begin. "Do people ever make judgments about you based on how you look?" I ask.

A few of the kids nod knowingly. "Sometimes people call me Four-Eyes," one boy with glasses pipes up. The little girl sitting next to him chimes in: "Last week someone made fun of my shirt at school. She said it was ugly." The kids take turns sharing their experiences, and it breaks my heart to hear that almost every one of them has already dealt with being judged by their appearance in one way or another.

"But do you know," I say, now excited to share this lesson, "that God doesn't look at what other people look at? God doesn't see our clothes or our hair or our glasses or our big ears. God looks at our hearts."

We take turns sharing again, but this time I ask each of the kids to share something about themselves that no one would know just by looking at them. "Maybe you are a kind sister, or maybe you're a really good artist, or maybe you are awesome at soccer." They can hardly wait to share the good parts of themselves, the things their friends at Sunday school might not know, and as we talk about David and Samuel and about how God chose David based on what was in David's heart, I can tell that the message is sinking in.

I love these kids, and suddenly I realize again what an amazing blessing and privilege it is to have the opportunity to touch their lives, if only just a little. *Thank you, God*, I silently pray, *for bringing me here today. Thank you for these kids and for this moment.* I'm almost certain I have gotten more out of this lesson than they have, but then again, that's not such a surprise. The simple and beautiful truth is that we get more when we give.

Less Greed

We usually have no trouble spotting the greediness in the people around us. That friend with the insatiable need for just a little bit more, an ever-bigger slice of the pie. That family member who refuses to share, even just a little. Sometimes our vision of greed is limited to that Ebenezer Scrooge character sitting alone in the corner, counting his piles of money while those around him starve.

It's not always easy to spot that same selfishness in ourselves.

But greediness comes in many different forms, and

our own greed often has nothing to do with money. It's not always easy to be generous. For most of us, our natural instinct is keep our resources, our talents, our love, and our money clutched to our chests in tightly clenched grips. When it comes right down to it, *we don't want to share.* And why would we? Sharing might mean there is less for us. We could run out. We could get shortchanged. We might get less, have less, *be* less. And so we are stingy.

If we were being totally honest with ourselves, how would we answer the following questions?

- **Am I stingy with my time?** Do I choose to spend my precious minutes each day focused on my own pursuits and desires, or do I purposefully carve out time in my day to do things for others?

- **Am I stingy with my effort?** Do I let others do the heavy lifting while I sit back and enjoy the fruit of their labor, or am I willing to dig in and get my hands dirty when necessary?

- **Am I stingy with my support?** Do I refuse to get involved or participate in a cause that might require some sacrifice on my part, or am I willing to stand up for what I know is right, even when it is messy or unpopular?

- **Am I stingy with my spiritual growth?** Do I look at my church involvement in terms of how I can be fed rather than how I can serve, or am I willing to help out and serve where needed, even in a lowly or humble position?

- **Do I reserve the best for myself?** Do I pick and choose what I want first and then give to those around me, or do I give first without worrying whether there will be enough for me?

- **Am I stingy with my kindness?** Do I purposely cut others down when I could be building them up? Do I withhold smiles and laughter from strangers when I could be giving them freely?

- **Am I stingy with my love?** Do I place conditions or strings on my friends and family, equating my love with their performance, or do I love freely and fully and generously, regardless of whether it is earned?

- **Am I stingy with my finances?** Am I willing to open my wallet and give generously to those in need, even when it means there might be less for myself? Do I tithe?

- **Do I forgo future gain for instant gratification?** Do I consistently make decisions I will regret later, such as overeating or overspending, because I know it will feel good right now?

- **Do I consistently ask, "What's in it for me?"** Am I motivated to act based only on what I can get rather than on how I can serve and impact the people around me?

The truth is that our greedy, selfish hearts will never be satisfied, at least not by the things of this world. We live in a culture that is totally immersed in a me-first mentality. *Do What Feels Good* and *It's Okay to Be Selfish* and *I Choose Me* are common battle cries, plastered on magnets and bumpers stickers. We buy into the lie that if we want it, we should have it—and we shouldn't have to share. We are concerned, first and foremost, with making sure we get our fair share. And while it is easy to spot that me-first attitude in others, I would dare to bet we are all at least a little stingy in one form or another.

Even so, we are called to live a different way. In fact, the Bible is full of stern warnings against greed and selfishness:

> Do not love the world or anything in the world. If anyone loves the world, love for the Father is not in them. For everything in the world—the lust of the flesh, the lust of the eyes, and the pride of life—comes not from the Father but from the world. The world and its desires pass away, but whoever does the will of God lives forever.
>
> 1 JOHN 2:15–17

> The greedy stir up conflict,
> but those who trust in the LORD will prosper.
>
> PROVERBS 28:25

> Put to death, therefore, whatever belongs to your earthly nature: sexual immorality, impurity, lust, evil desires and greed, which is idolatry. Because of these the wrath of God is coming.
>
> COLOSSIANS 3:5–6

Instead, we are called to live lives of abundant, overflowing, extreme, *totally irrational* generosity. We are called to love and to serve as Christ loved and served us, to love our neighbors as we love ourselves. That kind of love and that kind of service don't really make a whole lot of sense, at least not in today's world. But again, the Scripture is clear on what is required of us:

Honor the LORD with your wealth,
with the firstfruits of all your crops.

PROVERBS 3:9

"Give to everyone who asks of you, and if anyone takes what belongs to you, do not demand it back. Do to others as you would have them do to you."

LUKE 6:30–31

"In everything I did, I showed you that by this kind of hard work we must help the weak, remembering the words the Lord Jesus himself said: 'It is more blessed to give than to receive.'"

ACTS 20:35

Each of you should use whatever gift you have received to serve others, as faithful stewards of God's grace in its various forms.

1 PETER 4:10

Remember this: Whoever sows sparingly will also reap sparingly, and whoever sows generously will also reap generously. Each of you should give what you have decided in your heart to give, not reluctantly or under compulsion, for God loves a cheerful giver.

2 CORINTHIANS 9:6–7

You, my brothers and sisters, were called to be free. But do not use your freedom to indulge the flesh; rather, serve one another humbly in love. For the entire law is fulfilled in keeping this one command: "Love your neighbor as yourself."

GALATIANS 5:13–14

This call to give freely of our money, of our resources, of our time and talents, and of our hearts is not a request; it is a mandate. Generosity is not an option; it is a duty. Loving our neighbors as ourselves is not a onetime act; *it is a way of life.* Service is a state of mind. It requires a change in our hearts and minds that mirrors the one we read about in Philippians:

> Therefore if you have any encouragement from being united with Christ, if any comfort from his love, if any common sharing in the Spirit, if any tenderness and compassion, then make my joy complete by being like-minded, having the same love, being one in spirit and of one mind. Do nothing out of selfish ambition or vain conceit. Rather, in humility value others above yourselves, not looking to your own interests but each of you to the interests of the others.
>
> In your relationships with one another, have the same mindset as Christ Jesus:
>
> Who, being in very nature God,
> > did not consider equality with God something
> > > to be used to his own advantage;
> > *rather, he made himself nothing*
> > > *by taking the very nature of a servant …*

PHILIPPIANS 2:1–7, emphasis mine

This shift in attitude can only come through prayer. If we

are to become like-minded with Christ, we must continually pray for him to change our hearts and minds. A world that glorifies greed will always want us to be selfish, but Christ calls us to a different path. And the secret the world doesn't know is that *Christ's generosity will always be far more abundant than anything we could ever offer.* The more we give, *the more we are filled* with his love, his joy, and his peace.

Giving of Our Time and Talents

We often think of generosity only in terms of monetary gifts. Those who are willing to write the checks are the generous ones. But that is not exactly true. As we've already discovered, generosity starts in our hearts and minds, with Christlike humility and an eagerness to *serve.* I dare to bet that each of us has at least one special gift or talent or ability to offer. The reality is that getting our hands dirty in the trenches is usually far more difficult than simply making a donation and walking away.

When was the last time you stopped to think about how you are serving others in your community, your church, your child's school, your neighborhood, or even in your own family? When was the last time you made time to volunteer, especially when it meant taking on a thankless job or getting little or no recognition for your efforts? Sometimes our biggest barrier to service is that we just don't know what to do. Ruth Stafford Peale once stated that her life's motto was to "find a need and fill it"—and that philosophy is a great start. Once you start looking, you'll realize there is an almost endless list of ways to serve.

Here are a few practical ideas for ways to give of your time and talents:

IF YOU LIKE TO COOK OR BAKE

- Deliver a meal to a sick friend, a neighbor, or a shut-in.
- Bake cookies for your local firefighters, police officers, teachers, or other public servants.
- Volunteer to cook in a local soup kitchen or women's shelter.
- Provide and serve a meal for your church's youth or children's program.
- Send a care package to a college student or soldier.

IF YOU ARE GOOD WITH CHILDREN

- Become a Big Brother/Big Sister.
- Volunteer with a local youth organization.
- Become a tutor at an afterschool program.
- Volunteer to read at the local library or school.
- Become a parent helper in your child's classroom.
- Volunteer in the church nursery.

IF YOU LOVE ANIMALS

- Help an elderly neighbor by caring for their pet.
- Volunteer at the local animal shelter.
- Volunteer at a local wildlife center.

IF YOU CAN SING OR PLAY AN INSTRUMENT

- Sing in the church choir or play in the church band.
- Offer free music lessons for underprivileged kids.
- Sing or play for a local nursing home or school.

IF YOU ARE AN EXTROVERT

- Visit with residents at a local nursing home or assisted living facility.
- Become a bell ringer for the Salvation Army at Christmastime.
- Serve food at a local shelter.
- Volunteer at a local thrift shop.
- Teach a class.

IF YOU ARE AN INTROVERT

- Volunteer to shelve books at the local library.
- Volunteer in the stockroom of your local food pantry.
- Join a one-on-one "friendship" program for senior citizens in your community.
- Donate blood.
- Write encouraging notes or cards to teachers, friends, neighbors, soldiers, prisoners, or other people you know who may be feeling lonely or discouraged.

IF YOU ARE ATHLETIC OR OUTDOORSY

- Volunteer to help with Special Olympics in your area.
- Volunteer with the local park service.
- Volunteer to help with landscaping or grounds maintenance at your church or other local nonprofit organization.
- Become a coach or volunteer with a local youth sports program.
- Volunteer to work in a local community garden.

IF YOU ARE GOOD WITH TOOLS OR CRAFTS

- Volunteer for Habitat for Humanity or similar organizations.
- Help elderly neighbors or church members with home maintenance.
- Volunteer to help with decorations for a church or school fund-raiser or event.
- Make quilts or blankets to donate to shelters.

This list is supplied simply to get you started. Hopefully, once you start examining your own gifts, talents, personality, and passions, you will discover there are many ways to share them with the world. Make the giving of your time a priority, and the opportunities to serve will always present themselves.

Giving of Our Hearts

While the giving of our time and talents is essential, I often think the hardest thing for us to give—especially to those closest to us—is our own hearts. For whatever reason, whether we are scared of being rejected, angry at past wrongs, or simply too busy to even realize we are doing it, we withhold our love and kindness and encouragement from the friends and family closest to us. We forget that when Jesus told us to *love our neighbors as ourselves*, he wasn't necessarily talking about the stranger on the side of the road or the child in need half a world away. *Our neighbors are the people right in front of us.*

The opportunity to serve those in front of us is so constant that often we don't even recognize it. The seemingly bottomless requirements of our spouses and children feel like an obligation, an annoyance, a chore. We grow tired of the constant nature of all those requests, throwing up our hands and crying out in frustration, "Don't you ever stop needing things?"

But they don't, and they won't.

And this is our single greatest opportunity to give.

All the other secrets we've talked about in this book lead to this. Choosing contentment and finding our sweet spot, setting goals and managing our time, gaining control over our finances and telling our money where to go, decluttering our lives, keeping a tidy house, and even realizing that some of the best things in life are free all bring us right back home—to them, *the people right in front of us.*

So how do we give of our hearts? How do we serve in love within our very own homes? Here are some ideas:

- **Spend time in prayer and quiet reflection each day.** It is so easy to get so caught up in the day-to-day needs of our family that we forget how to serve them joyfully. Taking a few moments each morning to pray individually for each member of our family, as well as to pray for guidance on how to best serve them, can make all the difference in our attitude. Giving ourselves quiet time is also a great opportunity to recharge our own batteries so we are ready to serve.

- **Offer genuine encouragement.** Make it a point to be your spouse or your child's biggest cheerleader. Pay attention to the goings-on of their day-to-day life; find out what happened in their school or workday; meet their friends or colleagues; and understand their goals and ambitions. Celebrate their successes, and lift them up when they are discouraged.

- **Be gentle.** Protect the tender spirits of your children and your spouse by working to eliminate harshness from your speech and demeanor. Speak quietly and respectfully, and use kind words even when you are angry. *Especially* when you are angry!

- **Show grace.** Our children will inevitably disappoint us or hurt our feelings or do something wrong, and while they do need to be corrected and parented, they also need our grace and forgiveness. Likewise, our spouses often have the unique ability to wound us or let us down like no other person on the planet, but harboring bitterness only makes things worse. Instead, be willing to forgive and forget without harboring a grudge or resentment.

- **Show physical affection.** Make an effort to touch your kids and spouse each day in a loving way, whether it be a cuddle in the morning, an arm around the shoulder, a kiss on the cheek, or just holding their hand for a moment. Don't be stingy with your hugs, and don't withhold sex.

- **Be generous.** Give freely and generously of your time, your energy, and your resources. Do those basic things that make your family happy, such as taking care of the house or cooking meals, and do them with a joyful spirit. Help out without being asked and without expecting anything in return.

- **Slow down.** Have you ever stopped to count how many times in a day you tell your child or spouse to hurry? Stop rushing and take the time to enjoy the little things in life. If you are overcommitted, then be intentional about eliminating the things that don't need to be done so you can have more time to just be.

- **Have fun.** Laugh, be silly, and play games with your family. Go for walks or bike rides, or play together at the park. Spend a day at the beach, or build a fort in your living room. Do something completely unexpected, just for fun.

Becoming like-minded with Christ means adopting a servant's heart, both in our communities and in our own families. It is not always easy to be generous, especially in a world that tells us to keep the best for ourselves. Give anyway. It can be impractical and inconvenient to find the time to serve, and sometimes the giving of our resources can even feel like a hardship. Give anyway. It can feel like a burden to serve our families in love day in and day out, with little thanks and no recognition. Serve anyway.

In the end, it is these words of Paul to Timothy, which I quoted in chapter 1, that we ultimately come back to:

> But you, man or woman of God, flee from all this, and pursue righteousness, godliness, faith, love, endurance and gentleness. Fight the good fight of the faith. Take hold of the eternal life to which you were called ...
>
> Do not be arrogant or put your hope in wealth, which is so uncertain, but put your hope in God, who richly provides us with everything for our enjoyment. Do good, be rich in good deeds, and be generous and willing to share. In this way you will lay up treasure for yourself as a firm foundation for the coming age, *so that you may take hold of the life that is truly life.*
>
> 1 TIMOTHY 6:11–12, 17–19,
> emphasis mine, some verses paraphrased

The Good Life is one of service. It is based on *who we are* rather than what we have. It requires us to reject the lies of a society consumed with stuff and calls us instead to store our treasures in heaven. It is not for the faint of heart, and it is not always easy. It requires diligence and self-discipline, sacrifice and delayed gratification. It requires humility and prayer and generosity. But friends, despite all of this, the Good Life is worth the effort. It is worth any hardship and any cost, because it is the life that is truly life. The Good Life is eternal.

Won't you join me there?

CHALLENGE: **Share the Good Life**

Take an honest look at your own willingness to give. Are there areas in your life where you are stingy? Are you reluctant to give of your time or effort? Do you withhold love and affection? Are you sometimes cold and aloof when you could be showing kindness? Make a list of three areas in your life where you could stand to be more generous.

Next, take a look at how much you are currently giving of your time and talents to your church or community. How many hours a week or month do you spend volunteering or doing service work? Could it be more? Make a plan to volunteer or serve sometime in the next month.

Finally, look at how you are serving those people closest to you. Are you currently giving the best of yourself to your spouse and children? Write down three goals for making improvements in this area.

Notes

1. Committee to Protect Journalists, "10 Most Censored Countries," http://cpj.org/reports/2012/05/10-most-censored-countries.php# runners-up (accessed March 25, 2014).

2. World Hunger Education Service, "2013 World Hunger and Poverty Facts and Statistics," www.worldhunger.org/articles/Learn/ world%20hunger%20facts%202002.htm (accessed March 25, 2014).

3. World Health Organization, "Access to Essential Medicines," in *The World Medicine's Situation*, http://apps.who.int/medicinedocs/en/d/ Js6160e/9.html (accessed March 25, 2014).

4. "What Percentage of the World's Population Own a Car?" http:// wiki.answers.com/Q/What_percentage_of_the_world's_population_ own_a_car (accessed March 25, 2014).

5. Homeless World Cup Foundation, "An Estimated 100 Million People Worldwide Are Homeless," www.homelessworldcup.org/content /homelessness-statistics (accessed March 25, 2014).

6. Carrie Bay, "Job Loss Could Put One in Three Out of Their Home," September 30, 2011, http://dsnews.com/job-loss-could-put -one-in-three-homeowners-out-of-their-home-2011-09-30/ (accessed March 25, 2014).

7. Brad Plumer, "Here's Why 1.2 Billion People Still Don't Have Access to Electricity," May 29, 2013, www.washingtonpost.com/blogs/ wonkblog/wp/2013/05/29/heres-why-1-2-billion-people-still-dont -have-access-to-electricity/ (accessed March 25, 2014).

8. Water.org Facts, "Millions Lack Safe Water," http://water.org/ water-crisis/water-facts/water/ (accessed March 25, 2014).

9. Fred Whelan and Gladys Stone, "Lou Holtz's Compelling Quest to Do 107 Things Before He Died," December 9, 2010, www.huffington post.com/fred-whelan-and-gladys-stone/lou-holtzs-compelling-que_ b_794675.html (accessed March 25, 2014); "Lou Holtz 107 Goals," http://coachhuey.com/thread/5410 (accessed March 25, 2014).

10. Lewis Carroll, *Alice's Adventures in Wonderland* (1865; repr., New York: Simon & Schuster, 2000), 70–71.

11. Brian Tracy, *Eat That Frog!: 21 Great Ways to Stop Procrastinating and Get More Done in Less Time*, 2nd ed. (San Francisco: Berrett-Koehler, 2007).

12. Charles Duhigg, *The Power of Habit: Why We Do What We Do in Life and Business* (New York: Random House, 2012).

13. Country Financial Security Index, "'Perception Gap' Instills False Sense of Financial Security," May 15, 2012, www.countryfinancial securityblog.com/cfsi-full-may-2012/ (accessed March 25, 2014).

14. Grayson Bell, "Overspending in America—The Sad Truth," January 2013, www.debtroundup.com/overspending-in-america-the -sad-truth/ (accessed March 25, 2014).

15. "Compulsive Buying Disorder," *Wikipedia*, http://en.wikipedia .org/wiki/Compulsive_buying_disorder (accessed March 25, 2014).

16. Heather Hatfield, "Shopping Spree, or Addiction?" *Web*MD, www.webmd.com/mental-health/features/shopping-spree-addiction (accessed March 25, 2014).

17. "Men, Women Have Similar Rates of Compulsive Buying, Stanford Study Shows," http://med.stanford.edu/news_releases/2006/ september/shopping.html (accessed March 25, 2014).

18. Tara Struyk, "Sneaky Strategies That Fuel Overspending," February 26, 2009, www.investopedia.com/articles/pf/07/overspending.asp (accessed March 25, 2014).

19. Dennis Jacobe, "One in Three Americans Prepare a Detailed Household Budget," www.gallup.com/poll/162872/one-three-americans -prepare-detailed-household-budget.aspx (accessed April 8, 2014).

20. USDA Center for Nutrition Policy and Promotion, "Official USDA Food Plans: Cost of Food at Home at Four Levels, U.S. Average,

November 2013," www.cnpp.usda.gov/Publications/FoodPlans/2013/
CostofFoodNov2013.pdf. To find the latest updated food costs, see
USDA Center for Nutrition Policy and Promotion, "Cost of Food at
Home: U.S. Average at Four Cost Levels," www.cnpp.usda.gov/USDA
FoodCost-Home.htm. This chart offers a helpful baseline by which to
judge your grocery budget, because it shows four categories of spending
—thrifty, low cost, moderate, and liberal.

Living Well Spending Less®

Now that you've discovered the 12 Secrets of the Good Life, wouldn't it be nice to have a place to connect with others and to gather practical tips and accountability in a supportive atmosphere?

LWSLeveryday.com is that place.

Between the active community forum, inspiring interviews, live Q&A sessions, and limited edition downloads, LWSL Everyday will encourage, empower, and inspire you to seek—and find—the Good Life every single day

As a member of LWSL Everyday, you will:

- ✔ Get real-life accountability to help you set and achieve your financial and personal goals.
- ✔ Find new ideas for saving money and living well on a budget through inspiring behind-the-scenes interviews with your favorite authors.
- ✔ Gain exclusive access each month to beautifully designed, limited edition downloads.
- ✔ Connect with Ruth and get honest answers to your hardest questions in a monthly live webinar.

Your community is waiting.

Join us today at www.LWSLeveryday.com